The Golden Present

The Golden Present

Daily Inspirational Readings by Sri Swami Satchidananda

Integral Yoga® Publications
Yogaville, Virginia

Other books by Sri Swami Satchidananda:

Beyond Words
Kailash Journal
Guru and Disciple
To Know Your Self
Integral Yoga Hatha
The Healthy Vegetarian
Peace is Within Our Reach
The Living Gita: The Complete Bhagavad Gita
The Mother is the Baby's First Guru
The Yoga Sutras of Patanjali
(translation and commentary)
The Yoga Sutras of Patanjali
Pocket Edition
Integral Yoga Hatha booklet
(with audio cassette instruction)
Integral Yoga Meditation booklet
(with audio cassette instruction)

Books about Sri Swami Satchidananda:

The Master's Touch
Sri Swami Satchidananda: Apostle of Peace
(biography)

We are ever grateful to those whose generous Wisdom Offerings made the printing of this book possible.

Printed in the United States of America.
Library of Congress Cataloging-in-Publication Data
Satchidananda, Swami.
The Golden Present.

1. Spiritual life. 2. Devotional calendars.
I. Title.
BL624.S255 1987 294.5'43 86-33770
ISBN 0-932040-30-6

Integral Yoga® Publications
Satchidananda Ashram — Yogaville
Buckingham, Virginia 23921 U.S.A.

Published 1987. Second Edition 1989.

Acknowledgements

My heartfelt thanks are due to all of those who contributed in ways large and small to publishing this volume of daily readings.

My devoted student, Swami Hamsananda Ma, lovingly and patiently transcribed all of these entries, and prepared the manuscript. The eminent designer, Peter Petronio of Paris, France, generously contributed the design and cover art, based on the photograph taken by Tom Kelley, Sr. The photograph on the back cover was taken by Robert Altman.

Special thanks are also due to the dedicated staff of Integral Yoga® Publications: Swami Sharadananda Ma, Swami Premananda Ma, Swami Prakashananda Ma, Abhaya Thiele, Rev. Janaki Carrera and Bhaktan Bennetta; and Prema Serre, Gretchen Uma Knight and Swami Krupananda Ma of the art department.

The beautiful original drawings that introduce each month were donated by the artist, Maithreya Stillwater.

My appreciation and blessings to them all for their painstaking efforts.

Foreword

It has been a great honor to have worked on this project. With a grateful heart, may I offer humble thanks to my holy master, Sri Swami Satchidananda, on behalf of all who have received benefit from his teachings.

He has said, "Think of my teachings and try to apply them in your life. Then I am with you always. Because it is the teachings that are the teacher." It is my experience that if I follow any of the teachings of Sri Gurudev, I can be perfectly happy and peaceful. The teachings embody the truth that is found in all religions. One simply cannot go wrong following them. They work. Within these pages are what I would call the "cream" of Sri Gurudev's teachings, or the keys to the Kingdom. He has given us all we need; the rest is up to us. True peace is possible for every one of us.

May the entire creation be filled with peace and joy, love and light. OM Shanthi, Shanthi, Shanthi.

Swami Hamsananda Ma
Satchidananda Ashram — Yogaville

January

1 January

JUMP THE HURDLES

Life must be a challenge. Only then is it exciting. In an obstacle race, you are forced to surmount all the obstacles: to jump over the hurdles, go through barrels, crawl under rugs, climb over walls.

What would happen if, to avoid all that, you went around all the obstacles and asked for the winner's cup? Would they give it to you? No. They would say, "You must go back and face all the obstacles."

"Why?" you might ask. "If you are interested in giving me the cup, just give it."

"Sorry. You have to prove that you deserve it, that you worked for it."

Life is also a game, and we are proving ourselves. The challenge itself is joyous. If your life is always smooth, when you have great grandchildren you won't be able to sit back and tell them about all the adventures you had.

Imagine this conversation:

"You know, my child, when I was young like you this is what I did . . ."

"Oh! Grandpa, you did that? And then what happened?"

"I went to the jungle. I was chased by a tiger."

"Ahh! Ooo! Is that so?"

It will be so enjoyable to tell stories like that.

Instead if you just say, "Well, since my birth I just sat there at home. Nothing much happened," the kids will get up and walk away. They won't even listen to your story. So have something exciting to tell everyone later on. You will be so happy and proud.

Make your life as exciting as possible, but always think of it as fun. The adversities as well as the harmony should be enjoyable. Don't become sober and morose and have a castor oil face in the name of spirituality. Just be happy. Jump with joy. Even if you make a mistake, say, "Hey, I did this? Great! What a wonderful lesson I learned!" If you really want to, you can make everything fun.

THE WORLD WILL BE A FANTASTIC PLACE

There is a simple proverb told in the countryside of South India. If two good people coming from opposite directions are walking on the same narrow footpath, there will be three roads. If there is one good person, there will be two roads. If both are bad people, there will be only one road.

Probably this needs a little explanation. If both of the people are good, both will give room for the other one to walk on the path. That means they will create two more paths, emptying the center one. There will be three paths and they will comfortably pass, smiling at each other.

If there is one good fellow and one bad fellow, the good fellow will move out of the way and give room on the path for the bad fellow. So there will be two paths.

When both are bad fellows, they will come and push each other. "Hey, you! Get out!" "No, no, no! You get out!" There will be only one path.

The moral of the story is this: If you want peace, forget yourself. Think of the benefit of the other fellow first. "How can I serve *you* ? How can I make *you* comfortable?" That's the way it should be. Giving brings harmony. Love and give, love and give. Think of the other person first. With this kind of attitude, the whole world will be a fantastic place.

3 January

SURRENDER AND FREE WILL

God wants proof that you are totally surrendering yourself to Him. Tests will come. If you fail the tests then your surrender is not complete. If your surrender is complete, no matter what test comes you will pass it. Once you pass the tests, you don't have to worry about anything that happens in your life, because you are not responsible for your actions. Whatever comes, comes from God. Whatever goes is taken away by God.

It's not that easy in the beginning because your ego will not allow you to surrender this way. Until you become the master of the ego and give yourself into the hands of God, the ego will even create doubts in you.

You might ask, "Then what is free will?" Free will means you are free to take responsibility into your own hands or to give it into the hands of God. If you take the responsibility yourself, after going through all these problems, difficulties and turmoil, you will finally say, "I am tired, God. I'm not going to try to handle this anymore. I know I cannot. So the best thing is for me to put the reins in Your hands. Let me take the back seat. You drive."

There comes a time like that. That's when your ego has been completely cleaned. Then, even though it might appear to others that you are doing something, you will know that you are not doing it. You are being made to do it.

It is very difficult to have that kind of total surrender to God because the ego enjoys its supremacy. It won't give up that easily; there will be a big fight. You have to prove your capacity.

4 January

REAL LOVE IS POSSIBLE

Don't love only your fellow humans. Love everyone and everything equally. All things are your fellow beings, not only humans.

By loving everything, you are really loving yourself. Everything is nothing but the expression of yourself. If you stand in front of a mirror, you love that reflection. You smile at it and it smiles at you. In the same way, the whole world is your projection. You love because you are made of love; not because you have to love. The scriptures say to love your neighbor as your Self. You don't love your neighbor as an individual; you love that person as your Self.

That means you have to see your Self in the other person. Real love is possible only when you see everything as your own expression. All others are none other than you; they just appear to be different. We always need to go beyond the name and form. When we rise above the worldly limitations, we will find that the essence is the same.

5 January

BECOME A USEFUL INSTRUMENT

The essence of yoga and all the faiths and traditions is to be easeful in body, peaceful in mind, and useful in life. The aim of yoga is to make the body healthy and the mind tranquil and pure. With a pure mind and a healthy body, you become a useful instrument for God.

6 January

HAVE FUN AND PLAY YOUR PART

As long as you are in the world playing a part in this big drama, use the makeup and costumes, but don't get caught in your part. Have fun and play that part until the curtain falls.

Many people finish their part even in the midst of the drama. Once their part is over, they make their exit. Then they don't come back to the stage again. On the world's stage, many of us finish our job and leave, but the drama continues. Maybe the hero, the heroine and the villain will continue throughout, and be the last people to leave the stage. In the meantime, many extras come and go. We are probably all extras. Remembering this will help to keep the ego a little bit soft.

7 January

SILENCE

The person who really experiences the Truth will be more silent than others. Silence is the edge of the experience. To be humble, to be as quiet and silent as possible, is a sign of great wisdom. Wise people don't speak much. Just a few words here and there is enough. They don't need to say more than that. People learn just by seeing them and by sitting in their presence.

GOD IS NOT A FOOL

Question: How can we develop service as an instinctive, natural habit in our lives?

Sri Gurudev: By knowing that you are always serving. You don't need to develop anything. Simply know that you are not doing anything other than serving.

God sent you, and He must have had a purpose for sending you. He is not a fool. He will use you to fulfill His purpose. When He is not using you, you should not think, "Oh, I am no use at all. I am just sitting and doing nothing." That means that you forgot who is in charge. Your attitude should be, "Maybe God is just not using me now."

We are all tools in the hands of God. He brought us here to be used and He is literally using every one of us. It is God's energy that is in us. God is using me to say these things, and God is using you to listen. In a way, God is speaking and God is listening. It's not that I am in any way a great master, literate and enlightened, and you are all fools. No. It is simply that on this dramatic stage God is having me sit here and say something, and He is having you sit there listening. I know that it is God making me sit here and making you sit there. If you don't know it, that is the problem.

WHEN YOU THINK OF GOD

Saint Ramalingam once said, "When I repeat God's name, it is not only my tongue that repeats it; my whole body, my bones, my flesh repeat it. I feel that everything is melting."

Imagine that your beloved friend or partner went away somewhere and after five years he or she is returning. You are waiting at the airport and watching the customs gate as the passengers come in. The minute you even catch a glimpse of your loved one, how your heart pounds. Have you ever experienced that?

You should experience at least that much when you think of God. If that happens on the ordinary, physical level, imagine how much greater it is at the higher levels. So you should develop that. You *can* develop that. That is the purpose behind constant repetition of the mantram, constant remembrance through prayer.

HEALTH IS YOUR BIRTHRIGHT

Don't think that Hatha Yoga is just for athletes or for young people. It is written in the ancient yoga scriptures: "Anyone who practices yoga properly and sincerely becomes a *siddha*—an accomplished one—be he young or old, weak or strong, or even very elderly or sickly. From prince to peasant, child to grandparent, ailing to robust—all can practice these yoga postures and get maximum benefit."

Health is your birthright, not disease; strength your heritage, not weakness; courage, not fear; bliss, not sorrow; peace, not restlessness; knowledge, not ignorance. The person with health and strength of body, soundness of mind, with morality and spirit is a real gem among all humanity. Such a one possesses the true treasure.

TRY THIS YOURSELF

The aim behind all the hatha yoga postures is to be able to sit in one steady, comfortable position for meditation. It is only in a steady posture that you can have a good meditation. A body filled with toxins, weak muscles and jumpy nerves will not be able to stay quiet for any length of time. But the hatha yoga postures eliminate the toxins and give strength and steadiness. When the body is healthy and supple, you can easily sit with the mind still and peaceful. As you begin to control the body and its movements, that control will carry over to the mind.

Try this yourself. Any time the mind is agitated, just sit quietly, not moving at all. Let the mind be as agitated as it wants. If your body is still, very soon the mind will calm down all by itself. Why? Because when there is no physical movement, the breath becomes slow; and the breath is the interconnection between mind and body. As the breath slows, the thought-making process slows down and the mind becomes calm.

The *asanas* or postures help to train the mind. Without purity of body, it is very difficult to purify the mind. Learn to live a natural life. First be physically at ease, and mental peace will follow. Live in a way that makes your body light, healthy and more supple. Then when you sit for meditation, you won't feel aches and pains and spend your time meditating on them.

12 January

IT IS SOMETHING SUPER

You should have a close personal relationship with God. That's why sometimes it's easier to have a personal representation of God than an abstract one. You can communicate better, you can look at the face, you can garland Him, you can feed Him. God is nameless, formless, abstract; you cannot simply go and hug space. That is why most people need a symbol. It can be whatever pleases you. Develop your relationship with that. Marry yourself to that representation of God. Think of it day and night. Treat that as your inseparable partner. Once you develop that kind of relationship you will soon begin to see that God is always there next to you. Even if you forget sometimes, He will remind you, "Honey, I am here. Don't worry."

Devotion cannot be compared with any other approach. It is something super. When you develop that kind of devotion you rise above all doubts. You feel the presence always with you, and you feel that you are totally protected. Develop that kind of devotion by your constant remembrance of the Divine.

13 January

YOU CAN INFLUENCE YOUR SURROUNDINGS

You can build up your strength to the point where you are not influenced by your surroundings; in fact, *you* can influence the surroundings instead. You can change the environment if you have the strength of mind; but even if your mind isn't that strong, you can still have the strength not to be affected by the environment.

Learning not to be affected is an important step. If you are influenced by a situation, how can you change it? If fifteen people are crying and you go there and join them in the crying, you have simply added one more miserable person; you have not done anything to benefit those people. Instead, if you are really strong and can maintain your own equanimity, all the fifteen people will be benefited by your strength.

14 January

REST AT THE TOP

Wherever you are, whatever you do, have discipline in your life. Discipline your mind, discipline your senses, discipline your body. When we want a big reward, we have to pay a big price. Nothing comes easily. Even for a few minutes of ego gratification, for climbing to the top of a mountain, so much effort is needed. How many months of great difficulties will you have to undergo to attain such a goal? How many times will you slip, get up, start, slip, get up, start again? At last you stand there at the top, plant your flag, and say, "I conquered Everest." You may have conquered Everest, but you can never rest there. In ten minutes you even have to come down. For that ten minutes' joy you worked so hard, you followed so many disciplines. Then it's over.

In the spiritual life, however, once you get to the top, you have reached Ever-rest. You *do* rest there, and you won't have to come down. You can even pull others up as well. But there are no shortcuts. A great price must be paid to reach that great goal. What is that price? Leading a selfless life.

WE ARE ALL LEARNING

Let us not deny anybody just because he or she follows a certain path or doesn't follow a certain path. Ultimately we are all learning. If anyone is interested in knowing what practices you are doing, talk about it; explain how you have benefited, but don't try to persuade another to do the same thing.

That is what is meant by the Biblical saying, "Ask and it shall be given." You don't have to go and teach anyone. If someone asks, simply share what you know. If that person wants to do the same thing, fine. If not, if he or she wants to follow another path, that's fine too. With such an attitude you will learn to love everyone, respect everyone, and there will be harmony in your life.

16 January

THAT IS THE BEST VICTORY

When we win a war, it is a one-sided victory. A true victory should be for the benefit of everyone. If it is your victory alone, you may win the war now, but your enemy will be waiting for another opportunity to fight and be victorious over you. How can you call it a real victory if you still have an enemy somewhere?

Instead, make your enemy your friend. That is the best victory. Such a victory is only won by non-violent means, by trusting and by showing love.

BOTH HAVE LESSONS TO LEARN

If you want to give some advice, your first duty is to look and see if that person will accept it, if he or she will be benefited by your saying something. If the person gets upset, it shows that you don't know how to say it gently in the proper way. In that case, *you* learn something from it: "Ahh, I made her angry. I should have known how to present the problem. It is her problem, but I have to learn how to present it in the right way. Maybe I put it bluntly and that is why she got upset." There are things for you to learn also. If your intention is to help someone but you fail to make him realize that you are helping him, it's your mistake. You can't blame him for that.

The giver of the help should remember certain things about how to give constructive suggestions. Stop and think, "Is this the right moment to discuss this? Am I presenting it in the proper way?" If you positively know that the person is not in a mood to receive it from you, wait until another time or start very gently. Then give that person time to think about it. Maybe at the spur of the moment the ego will come and say, "How dare you tell me that!" But when you go away, he or she will try to apply your advice. Remember there is a giver and a receiver; both have lessons to learn.

18 January

ANYTHING CAN ROLL DOWN

If you cannot control your ordinary, earthly, human nature, you are not going to realize the spirit. Control the tongue, control the eye, control the flesh, control the food. Why? Because we are rising above nature so that we will not be controlled by it. It should be under our control. Every discipline in life ultimately gives you strength to transcend the limitations of the senses.

A stone easily rolls downhill. Anything can roll down; but to bring something up is a difficult task. We are trying to raise ourselves up. If you throw something up, it comes back down. Why should it come back? Because the natural gravitation pulls it down. In the same way, our minds and bodies are constantly being pulled down toward the earth and we are trying to change that. We want to get the help of a rocket to go past the gravitational pull.

That is why we have all the disciplines. Without discipline, this ascent would not be possible at all. Even if one wire is loose or one conductor is weak, a rocket launch is postponed. We are all trying to launch our rockets. The mind is a rocket. The body is the launching pad. Your mind must be well-fueled and well-tuned, and then you must set fire. Ten, nine, eight, seven, six, five, four, three, two, one, zero! Launch yourself. Once you go beyond the gravitational pull, you transcend the mind. Realization comes only when you have a proper launching pad (body) and proper rocket (mind) to help push you beyond the gravitational pull.

At this point, the analogy ends, because you are not really launching yourself from here to somewhere else. Everything happens right where you are. Right here you can master the forces that pull you down. You don't have to shoot off somewhere, but you do have to discipline the mind and body. Only then can you command nature.

19 January

UTILIZE YOUR LOVE

Question: When we feel an extra surge of love from within, what can we do to keep that love flowing instead of being blocked up inside or focused all on one person?

Sri Gurudev: When you feel that extra surge of love, you have hundreds of opportunities to share it.

If you see a withering plant, immediately go and tend to it, take the weeds out, give it some nourishment and water. If you notice a pebble or a piece of glass on the road, love the person who would get cut by stepping on it and pick it up before anyone is hurt. You can show love to plants, to the road, to people, to animals. Let everything that is in your presence make use of that love. Be nice to all. Do something beautiful.

Let your love be a universal love. That is true love. Always do something good for all others, not just for people. When I say others, I mean even a little plant or a stone. Pour your love onto all those things.

Concern about the feelings of others and the happiness of others is real love. It's unfortunate that love is often limited to something physical. That's not love at all. Love is concern for others, doing good to everyone and everything. Utilize your love for the benefit of the Creation.

20 January

ACCEPT

Whatever comes, accept it as God's Will.

IT IS ALL YOU, YOU, YOU

The more you think of yourself—"What can I get?" "How much can I gain?" "What should I wear?" "What should I eat?" "What should I do?" "I! I! I!"—the more karma comes to you. We cannot avoid karma already accrued, but we can avoid the new ones by not doing anything for our sake. By always feeling, "Everything is being done through me by God. I am not doing anything for selfish purposes. I am doing everything for the sake of others, for the benefit of humanity in the name of God." That way all your actions become selfless service, *karma yoga*. You do not create any new karma that way.

You cannot exhaust all the accrued karma in one lifetime. You come only with what you can burn out in this life. When that is over, another group of karmas will come and you will be given another birth. Until all of it is exhausted, you will take on bodies. If you are lucky enough not to create any new karma, one day everything will be exhausted.

There is one way that it all can be burnt—all past, present and future karma. That is when you totally put yourself into the hands of God and say, "I am not the doer, I have not done anything. It is all You, You, You. You do whatever You want. It's not even *my* past karma. I made a mistake in thinking it was mine. I know it is all Yours. I simply put the label 'mine' on it, so I am suffering. Now I realize no action, and no reaction, was ever mine."

That is the ultimate realization. When you realize this, you rise above all the karma. You feel that you are not doing anything, and that you have never done anything. It's true. We have never done anything ourselves; we have no capacity to do anything ourselves. It is God who does everything.

So don't ever say, "I did it. That's mine. I earned it." Instead say, "God, it is all You. Even the thought is Yours. The energy is yours, functioning through this instrument. Nothing belongs to me. I am Thine, all is Thine, Thy will be done."

If we realize that, and if we live up to it, then no karma will ever bother us. We don't need to worry about anything.

22 January

NOTHING WILL BOTHER YOU

Nothing will bother you if your relationship with it is correct. Pain becomes evil because you don't like it. Nothing will bother you, no one will bother you, nothing will harass you if your attitude is right. What is the right attitude?

You should understand that no pain will come to you unless you do something to deserve it. Pain is not really that gracious; it will not just come by to visit. No. If we deserve something, whether good or bad, it will come to us. If we don't deserve it, nobody can hurt us. No pain can come to us. Deserving means we have done something wrong and through that pain we have to purge it out. Pain is a sort of purgation. Even if the whole world comes forward to give you pain, it cannot if you do not deserve it. But unfortunately we don't accept it that way. We simply say, "Ohh, I am all innocent. This guy just came and hurt me." It's wrong thinking. Pain has no interest in coming to you unless you have invited it. Understand the purpose of the suffering, and accept it.

WE DON'T LOSE ANYTHING

Don't think that you can do everything just by your own capacity alone. Know that there is a higher power, a grace, to help you; but you have to sincerely ask for it. Unless you ask, you won't receive it. Just by asking, you are opening yourself to that power. It's not that God is waiting for you to ask; God is not miserly. He is already giving, but we do not always receive.

The process of asking is itself opening; you cannot even ask without opening. So open your heart. Even if you can't open your heart to people, open your heart to God; then you will know how to open your heart to people also. Pray sincerely and trust in a higher power, trust in God. Many, many more things are wrought by prayer than the world dreams of. Let us believe in sincere prayer.

What we can achieve by ourselves is very little, but what we can achieve with the help of God is very great. We don't lose anything by giving ourselves to God. As the great saint Manickavasagar said, "I gave myself to You, Lord, and in return You gave Yourself to me. Who is gaining? With me You are not gaining anything. Just a useless thing, incapable of doing even a little. I'll be a burden to You, one more stomach to feed. But with You, I can do many things. If I have You, I have gained everything in the world. So You see, though You call it a fair business deal, You are really losing."

24 January

YOU CAN WIN NOBEL PRIZES

People talk a lot about God-realization and spirituality, but they don't realize how much they have to pay for it by their own effort.

You can become an Olympic champion and win all the gold medals. You can win Nobel Prizes. You can even become a statesman, a president, a multi-millionaire. It's all nothing. Anybody can do that, and people *are* doing it easily.

The real achievement comes in doing what an ordinary person cannot do. It takes an extraordinary person, an extraordinary mind, a superhuman to achieve the highest goal. If you are not willing to make the greatest effort, don't even think about the greatest goal. Think about some small goal: "All right, I want to get a medal." Or "I want to become famous." Or "I want to be rich."

The spiritual goal is the grandest goal, but people expect it to somehow happen overnight without any effort. There are people who have been working birth after birth toward this goal. It may take ten births, one hundred births, or it may happen tomorrow. If you really make up your mind about what you want, that's a start. It makes things easier.

It's not just a simple thing you are asking for. When somebody wanted to follow Jesus, what did he say? "Get rid of everything, give it to the poor. Take up your cross, and follow me." What does it mean? Give up everything. When you give up everything, you get everything.

25 January

YOU SHOULD ALWAYS CHOOSE PEACE

When anything comes to you, first ask yourself, “Will I be maintaining my peace by getting this, or will my peace be disturbed?” Ask that for everything. People you would like to be with, possessions you would like to acquire. It doesn’t matter what you want to do; strike that against the touchstone of peace. “Will this rob me of my peace?” If the answer is “Yes, you must choose peace or the other thing,” you should always choose peace. If the answer is, “My peace will not be disturbed by it,” okay, you can have that and still have your peace. That should be our aim.

26 January

REMEMBER HIS UNSEEN HAND ALWAYS

An individual's act is nothing but a part of a cosmic act. It's not that *you* are acting. You are made to act. Somebody made you with a purpose. Know that somebody has made you, somebody is making you work and somebody is going to make you stop. You are free to remember that or not. That's all.

If there is a request in our prayers it should be, "God, You are doing everything. Occasionally I think of that, I know it, but very often I forget it. I know that You are the one who makes me forget also; but please don't play that trick on me, because when You make me forget, I become egoistic, I become miserable. So please don't have fun with me like this. Help me to remember this always. I don't know if it is just for Your fun, or if You are testing me. I don't know why You are doing all this. All I know is I go through sufferings when I forget that. I have had enough of that suffering. Please help me to remember." That should be our prayer. To recognize His unseen hand always.

WITHOUT THAT, NOTHING IS GOING TO MAKE YOU HAPPY

You might have the entire world at your feet, all the money, all the material things, all the friends, all the name, all the fame, all the crowns; but unless you have peace you don't have a worryless life. What is the use of having all these things around you? Shun them. Care more for your peace than for these. Without that peace, nothing is going to make you happy. If you have peace, even without having anything else, you will be happy. That's what you call contentment. Accept God's will, "Whatever has to come will come. What will not come, will not come. Why should I worry about it?" I know some of you might say, "Then should I not do anything?" You should do something, yes. And if you allow yourself to be handled in that way, you will have plenty to do. You'll be doing much more than anyone else. At the same time, you'll be totally relaxed. Don't think that relaxation or peace comes by not doing anything. No. You'll be put to even greater use.

28 January

THEN NOBODY WILL LIE

Question: What is the proper attitude to have toward someone who is lying to me?

Sri Gurudev: When somebody lies to you, he or she is afraid of you. He is not courageous enough to tell what he feels. Be sympathetic and give the person confidence that he or she doesn't need to lie. Give people confidence; then nobody will lie.

29 January

WE CAN DO A LOT

Can we do something to stop all this nonsense between the United States and the Soviet Union? Yes, we can do a lot. Sincerely send good thought vibrations. Think loudly. Say, "We love you, our Russian brothers and sisters, and we know that you love us." Send loving vibrations and thoughts. Don't even think of war and send out fearful thoughts; the whole world is being bombarded by fearful thoughts. Even though there is reason for fear, the more we are afraid, the more we are sending those thoughts. The atmosphere is filled with that fear, and that alone will kill us. So instead send hope, love, trust. Every day take some time in your meditation to pray especially for the welfare of the entire world. Perhaps we do that already, but let us really *mean* it. "May auspiciousness be unto *all.*" *Feel* that. "May *peace* be unto all." Or you can make up your own phrases. Let us remember that a good thought is more powerful than a bomb. Arms cannot do anything against a good thought. So let us send out peaceful thought forms every day especially for this kind of understanding. That way we can all contribute toward the welfare of the globe.

30 January

NEXT TO THE ROSE, HE MADE A THORN

We should learn to use everything for good. God never made anything bad in this world. He made a rose, and next to the rose He made a thorn. You should know to take the rose and not put your hand on the thorn. The thorn has its purpose also; if you take away all the thorns, the rosebush will die. You need both the rose and the thorn. True knowledge is knowing how to use everything properly and for the benefit of all.

LORD, I KNOW YOU GAVE ME THIS STOMACHACHE

If you have absolute faith, you will always be happy and joyful even in the midst of suffering. You may have severe handicaps, but you can still be joyful.

When Tirunavukarasar, one of the well-known Saiva saints, was suffering from a stomachache, he said, "Lord, I know You gave me this stomachache. I don't know what I did to deserve it. Certainly I did something; but I don't remember what it is. Maybe it was even in a previous birth. But one thing I do know: You want me to trust You completely. Probably this is the only way You can make me do that. You are very kind to make me think of You. If You didn't love me, why would You even bother to give me this problem? You wouldn't even be thinking of me. The very fact that You thought of me makes me happy; because this has made me remember to think of you. When I experience pleasure, I may forget You; but when I experience pain, I can never forget You.

"I'm not asking You to get rid of it right away. Please just give me strength and continue to give me this problem until I completely purge out my karma. I know You are merciful. You want to bring out the beauty, the pure part of me, so You are simply rubbing and scrubbing me. It hurts sometimes, but I know that You would not unnecessarily hurt me. If there were another more simple way, You would certainly have done it that way. Probably my problem is too tough. So go ahead; do what You must. All I request is that You give me the strength and the understanding to accept it."

What a beautiful prayer. With this kind of approach, we can face any problem in life. Nothing will shake us, whether it is physical or mental, caused by people or caused by nature. We just need to have that absolute faith.

February

1 February

ULTIMATE HELP

On a pilgrimage you learn to depend on a higher source. You learn that you cannot depend on anything else for your safety or for your peaceful life. All other things, though they are around, can only help you to a certain extent. They are limited. The ultimate help comes from the God within.

2 February

NOTHING IS IMPOSSIBLE

God knows your breaking point. His purpose is not to break you. No, not at all. You simply don't know your own strength. You may think, "I've reached my limit. I can't do any more." If you couldn't do it, God would not be putting you into that situation. God knows you better than you know yourself.

Unfortunately He can't help you if you have doubt. Doubt and faith don't go together. If you have complete faith, nothing is impossible. Nothing. That kind of faith will not grow in an impure, selfish mind; so learn to be selfless. Trust in God and say, "Whatever I deserve, God will give me. Whatever I don't deserve, God will take away. Whatever I need, God will keep with me. The minute the need is over, He will remove it." If we have that kind of total trust, we will always maintain our peace.

3 February

THE REAL SPIRITUAL EXPERIENCE

Living and working together as one beautiful family with total love is God. People often ask me, "Why is it that I've been practicing all these years but I haven't realized God? I haven't had any experience." I don't know what it is that they are looking for. Do they mean they haven't been lifted off the floor a few inches? They haven't had any hallucinations? That's not the kind of spiritual experience you need. You may have some nice visions; you may see lights, hear sounds. But what is the benefit to others? Real spiritual experience means moving around with a smiling, loving face. That is spiritual. To see the spirit in others and to love everyone; to rise above these little differences of the lower nature and bring harmony wherever you are.

If you can't live harmoniously with others, what is the use of other spiritual experiences? Ultimately, everyone should love you. Keep that in mind: "I will live the kind of life that will make everybody love me, and I will love them." If that happens in your life, you will know that you are growing spiritually.

4 February

THE BEST COMPLIMENT

Question: What would be the greatest compliment a student could show you?

Sri Gurudev: The best compliment would be to make me see him or her experiencing all the joy and happiness and health that I experience. That's the best compliment. Not just mere words or praise. I want them to *live* that life. I want them to see in their life what I am experiencing, if not more. It will be better if it's more.

GOD IS ALL OF THESE AND MORE

God is "He" and "She" and "It" and even more than that. In the name of simplifying, we usually say "He" because that has been recognized as the so-called neutral pronoun. But God need not be a father. God can be a mother also. God can be a brother, a sister, a friend, a tree. God is everything.

God is Spirit, and Spirit is above all these distinctions. To realize God as Spirit is what is called spiritual practice. Unfortunately even in the spiritual life problems come up about male and female. Arguments about men and women don't belong in a church or synagogue or ashram. There should be no discrimination against one or the other. When you talk about the physical body, you are talking about flesh, blood and bone. Spirit is above all these things. If you are going to fight about male and female, don't call yourself a spiritual person. Spirit has no gender.

Still, we love the Spirit or God and want it to manifest in some form or other so that we can express our devotion. If you love the image of a father, let God come as a father to you. If you love the image of a mother, God can manifest as a mother for you. If you adore nature, call God by the name of Nature. God is all of these things and more.

LET US ALL REMEMBER THE REAL TRUTH

It doesn't matter what form you choose to worship. As long as your interest is in recognizing and realizing the presence of that Spirit, you can approach It in any form you like. If you don't care for any of the traditional forms that have been handed to us over the ages, you can create your own form and God will come to you as that. There is no limit to God's expression. God need not be put into only a few categories. God is ready to send Itself in any form that will help you to realize that Spirit. God is essentially nameless, formless, omnipresent. If you say, "God is omnipresent," then it is nonsense to say, "God is only this."

It is easy to say the words: "God is omnipresent, omnipotent, omniscient," but hard to fully understand. If we stop to think of the real meaning of the words, then all this limiting of God doesn't make any sense. However, our mental capacities are limited. The mind cannot truly understand the unlimited One. It is to give us something to focus on that we limit something that is unlimited. We need that help to go beyond the limitation and realize the One or God.

That is the reason for all the forms and names we use in worship. Whatever form or name we may choose, let us all remember the real Truth of the limitless, formless, omniscient, omnipresent, and omnipotent One behind them all.

7 February

THE ESSENCE OF YOGA

Let us talk a little about *samadhi*. In the yogic sense, we are talking about the transcendental state of enlightenment. But in India, normally if you say, "He has attained *samadhi*, " that means he has died and is buried. That is the normal connotation for that term. In a way, *samadhi* is like that. You are dead, yet you are alive. My Master Sri Swami Sivanandaji used to sing this song: "When shall I see Thee? When 'I' ceases to be." He was asking this question of the Lord. "Lord, when can I see You? I know that will be when 'I' ceases to be." That means that if the ego or "I" dies, you can truly live.

If the egoistic "I" goes away from you, you are free from the ego. You are clean, pure. At that stage you are fit to go to heaven, to experience the highest knowledge or the highest truth. That is what we call *samadhi*. This is the essence of all spiritual teachings and practices, no matter what the label. One can be a Catholic, a Protestant, a Jew, a Hindu, Buddhist, Moslem, or of any religion. Even if you don't have any faith at all or don't believe in any organized religion, it doesn't matter. That is not the criterion to have this realization. All you have to accomplish is to see that all selfishness goes away.

Where does the "I" dwell? In ego. Where does the ego live? In the mind. The ego is, in a way, the very source of mind. All the expressions of the ego, thinking, feeling, willing, could be put together under one term, "mind." If the mind gets completely purified, then it's no longer an obstruction to your experience of the Truth. When it is clean and clear, the mind doesn't color the appearance of the pure Self. It becomes a pure reflector of the Self to see its own true nature. That is the essence of spirituality.

YOU LEARN EVEN FASTER

If you make mistakes it doesn't matter. Make mistakes and learn. The best teachers are your own mistakes. You learn even faster by your mistakes. Once I was at a conference with the great modern scientist Buckminster Fuller. He stood up and said, "Friends, forget about all the 'Do this. Don't do that' business. Commit as many mistakes as possible, as soon as possible. You'll become great!"

It's true. Every failure is a stepping stone. Remember, though, that you can't use the same stone for each step. Every step should be on a new stone. That means you shouldn't keep on making the same mistakes. Learn well from each one. The problem with many people is that they commit the same mistake over and over. Even so, they will eventually learn from that mistake and move on. Experience is the best teacher.

9 February

YOUR WHOLE MIND SHOULD BE ON IT

When you do a thing, your whole mind should be on it. Success depends on your application of the mind. Without that concentration, it's a half-hearted job. Part of your mind will be here, part of it will be somewhere else. You cannot achieve success in anything that way. That is one reason for practicing meditation: to train the mind to stay focused on one thing at a time.

10 February

NOT EVERY HOLE HAS A SNAKE

We have to correct our vision. It's not only the eye that sees, but the "I" sees also. Sit in meditation and think, "Am I seeing things and people without any prejudice, or do I project my image?" We see not just the person, but our own prefixed notions. It's a very natural thing, and it's very hard to escape from that. When that happens, you have to question yourself: "Why am I seeing that person this way?"

A country proverb says, "Not every hole has a snake." You may happen to see a snake going into a hole; fine, remember that all holes are not free from snakes. But don't look for a snake in every hole you come across. See each one individually.

11 February

THE HIGHEST REALIZATION IS THAT

Everything is happening according to God's Will. Everything. God is behind everything. We are all puppets. He pulls a string, I raise my hand this way; another string, I raise my hand another way. He drops the string, my arm drops.

So we are all puppets. If we realize that, why should we worry about the role we are playing? If He wants you to play that part, play it. No part is big or small. Only by knowing this truth can you become great. It is immaterial where you are, what you are doing.

The great saint Thaimanuvar said, "Don't worry about which is better, monastic life or householder life. Both are equally good if only you know one secret. What is that secret? We are all tops. There is one Player. He simply winds the string around and pulls it, and then we spin. Depending on how tightly the rope is wound and how fast He plays, you rotate for a while and then you fall down."

It's not how you present yourself, what you call yourself, what you do for a job that's important. The most important thing is: Do you know that you are nothing but a top and that at any moment your swinging could stop? The highest realization is that. Know that every minute that great Presence is in you, functioning through you, and you are nothing but an instrument.

12 February

WE SHOULD BE ABLE TO OFFER OURSELVES

Not everyone can go out and serve physically. Those who have that capacity should do so. Those without that capacity can project their positive thoughts. In fact, thoughts are more powerful than actions. Many great sages and saints who live in caves and remote areas just sit and pray for others. Those positive suggestions spread all over the globe. Thoughts are more powerful; there is no doubt about it. Many contemplative monks, nuns, and other people sit and pray for the world.

Those who have the capacity to do something physical as well should take that opportunity. Mental, physical, material—do something in whatever way you can. That is why all those faculties have been given to you. They are not given just for your own use. Your physical strength, your material wealth, everything is given to you to be used for others. Of course that doesn't mean that you should not use it for yourself too; but the major part of it is to be offered to others. That's the way we should mold our lives. You should not think that you are living here for your own sake. We are here for the sake of everyone. On every plane we should be able to offer ourselves and our possessions for the benefit of humanity and the entire nature.

13 February

REAL LOVE MEANS YOU THINK OF THE WELFARE OF OTHERS

Question: How can I learn to love?

Sri Gurudev: Wanting to love itself is the beginning. And if you want to love, then you should know how to love. Real love means you think of the welfare of others. You do everything for the sake of others. You don't put yourself first. If others do something to you in return, it's all right; accept it, but don't look for it. If you look for it, you are setting up conditions. "Only if you love me in return or if you do this and this and that and that will I love you. Otherwise I will not."

All our problems are caused by this. We lose trust and become miserable when love is conducted like a business. You will not be happy with this kind of love. Don't worry about the other person. Whether it is between husband and wife or even between two friends, if your relationship is based on some gain from that person, you are never going to be happy. The other person cannot always give you what you want. So be content just to love.

14 February

EVERYBODY HAS A HEART

Everybody has a heart. You should know how to touch it. Behave in such a way that you can transform other hearts, melt them. Let that beautiful feeling come to the surface by your example. If you don't know how to touch the heart, it is your mistake and not the other person's mistake. Be patient; have strength. We tame even the wild animals, don't we? Bengal tigers walk like a little puppy. Cobras dance with joy. Can't we do something to a human being? Don't just put the blame on the other person.

15 February

THE DARKNESS WILL RUN AWAY

Question: How can you trick your mind into getting rid of a bad habit?

Sri Gurudev: How can you trick your baby so you can take away something that would hurt it? Suppose the baby is playing with something sharp. What kind of trick would you use? You would give her something nice to distract her.

In the same way, find some nice, positive habits. Present them to the mind. Admire them. "Oh, look how terrific this habit is. So useful. Something to be proud of." Certainly your little baby mind will jump to grab it. As soon as it jumps for the good habit, take away the bad one.

If you want to be rid of bad company, what should you do? Just get into good company; the bad company will automatically stay away. It's simple. You won't be available to the bad people because you will always be mingling with good people. That's a very good beginning toward a very high goal. Sri Patanjali calls it *pratipaksha bhavanam* —substituting positive thoughts for negative ones. Think of the opposite, develop the opposite. If you have hatred, develop love. That is the trick. You cannot simply beat a bad habit to get rid of it. That's like being in a dark room and beating the darkness, telling it to get out. Instead, just bring in a candle. Without even saying goodbye, the darkness will run away.

16 February

IF YOU CAN, HELP THEM

Question: How can one see oneself in someone who is nasty and violent?

Sri Gurudev: Think that once you too might have been like that. Now you have become a nice person. He or she will also grow that way. Give people time. Don't think we were all born saints and yogis. Every grown-up once crawled. Today's sinner is tomorrow's saint. Be sympathetic. Don't dislike such people. If you can, help them. If not, at least don't hate them. By being nasty and violent, they might even learn some good lessons. They will change one day. We have no right to condemn *anybody*.

Think to yourself, "Yes, I could have been like that at one time." Or, "I should not be like that. This person has performed a great service by clearly showing me what to avoid in myself."

There is always a positive way of looking at things.

17 February

UNIVERSE-ITY

The entire universe is a university. Everything and everybody is a professor to us. We constantly learn from everybody and everything. We learn even more through pain than through pleasure. Whether we want it to or not, the world will give us the experiences we need and make us grow.

DID YOU PRAY WITH TOTAL FAITH?

The only real help comes from God. Pray sincerely. A sincere prayer will certainly be answered. If your prayer is not answered, don't blame God for that. It simply means that you have not prayed enough. It's not just a question of the length of time. You may be praying for ten years and get nothing. Somebody else might pray for one minute and get everything. So the quality of the prayer is the important thing, how honestly, how sincerely you pray.

Suppose that even a whole-hearted prayer doesn't get answered. Then the question is, did you pray with total faith? If you offer a prayer with absolute faith in God, and if the prayer is not answered, will you lose that faith? It is true that all of your sincere prayers will be answered; but that does not mean you will necessarily be given what you want. The answer might be: "It's no good for you, my child. However much you cry, I can't give that to you because it will hurt you. Without knowing how to use it, you may hurt others also. It's dangerous." If you understand that and accept it, you prove that you trust in God.

Don't just trust in God when you get everything. If, out of one hundred requests, ninety-nine are denied, you should still have that faith. That will eventually lead you to a higher form of prayer where you don't request anything. You simply say, "Why should I ask You? The fact that I am asking You means that I think You don't know what I need. How ignorant I am. You know what is good for me; You know what is not good for me. Do whatever You want. Why am I even asking for something? Maybe You made me ask. Even the asking seems to be Your prompting. Because You wanted me to ask, I am asking. Still, I leave it to You to give it or not. Maybe You asked me to ask You; then You are going to say no to see whether I will accept it or not. Okay, I am ready for that also."

The more you trust God, the more you will get tested. Trust and testing go together.

19 February

WHAT IS IT THAT I AM DOING?

The simplest thing is to have faith. An ounce of faith moves mountains. The saint Ramalinga Swamigal used to say, "Lord, You are feeding me, so I am eating. Otherwise I wouldn't even be able to eat my food. Do You think I am eating with my capacity? No. You are feeding me. When You want me to eat, I eat. When You want me to sleep, I sleep. When You want me to see, I see. Without You, I cannot even see. When You want me to be happy, You make me happy. You make me dance, I dance. I'm just a puppet, and You pull the string. You do this to everyone; I'm not the only one. I know that it's all You. Many may not know that. Unfortunately, because of the ego, they think that they are moving by themselves. But still, the fact is that You are moving them. When that is so, what is it that I am doing? It's all You."

Once you realize that truth, your whole life will be totally different. You won't see anything other than peace and joy.

20 February

THE HEART WILL WIN

The heart should play an important role, not only in married life, but in all of our relationships: with friends, relatives, business associates, and even strangers. Even if the other person uses the head, you should use more heart. Remember, ultimately the heart will win; it might take time but it will win. If you really want to use your heart, you will be guided in that direction. God's guidance will be there. Pray more and trust in that higher force.

21 February

THERE IS A NATURAL GRAVITATION

Question: Why is it so difficult to be disciplined?

Sri Gurudev: That is part of nature. There is a natural gravitation that makes it easy to push things down, and hard to lift them up. That pull is there; but we have been given the capacity to face it and rise above it. That is discipline.

22 February

GO AHEAD

A good spiritual teacher should say, "This is the way I know. It is positively helpful. If you like, you are welcome to follow it."

Suppose you say, "I don't want to go that way. I want to go in the opposite direction."

The teacher will say, "All right. Go ahead. Do it."

Then you go in the wrong direction, bump against a wall and say, "Ahh. I made a mistake. It's the wrong direction. I'll go the other way." That's what experience means. Nature itself teaches us, allows us to make mistakes.

Didn't God allow Adam to eat the fruit? Though He said, "Adam, don't eat the apple," did He stop Adam when he reached for the apple? He certainly *could* have stopped him. Instead, He simply allowed Adam to make the mistake so that he would learn the lesson.

There should be freedom in learning. Each one learns in a different way. The duty of a teacher is to see if there are any impediments on the path, and clear them so that you can go on. He or she should help you to experience in your own way. By going here and there, and bumping into obstacles, you will very soon understand the truth: "Wherever I go, ultimately I end up with a problem. Every time I do something with my ego, it gets me into trouble. All these days I have been following my ego. Now I don't want to follow it anymore. I give up."

23 February

HAVE THAT COMPLETE TRUST

Question: How can you know if another person is telling you the truth?

Sri Gurudev: Until you positively know that he is telling a lie, trust that he is telling you the truth. If you always look at that person with suspicion, even the truth will look like a lie to you because that is what you are looking for. If you constantly look for lies, even the truth will look false to you. Have that trust. Even if all of a sudden you come across a situation where someone seems to have told a lie, don't immediately jump to that conclusion. Investigate well. Things are not necessarily what they seem. Make sure that you understand the situation correctly before drawing conclusions.

24 February

YOU CAN JUST TAP RIGHT INTO IT

Book learning is nothing compared to deeper learning. There is a fund of knowledge in nature itself. If your brain is clear, you can just tap right into it. You can easily find a solution for any problem. It's not anyone's monopoly. Everyone can do that.

25 February

THE PHYSICAL HELP IS LIMITED

What you call the spiritual master or teacher or guru is not the person. The guru is eternal. The guru's inspiration, the guru's force, the guru's divine energy, the guru's vibration will always be there guiding you, directing you. The help that can be given through the physical body is limited; on the spiritual level, the guru can help you much more. Always try to communicate at that higher level. In your practices, in your meditation, you should learn to communicate with the spiritual part of the guru.

The guru need not consciously give you blessings and teaching. If you are ready to receive it, even he cannot stop it. The more you follow the teachings, the more you have the guru's presence and communicate with the guru. The teaching is the guru. The teacher is only a vehicle.

If I am giving a talk, I am the one who is speaking, not the microphone. But you hear the talk through the microphone, through the speakers. The real speaker is the spiritual part that simply functions through *this* machine. For some time you might need the speaker, but you shouldn't depend on that always. Learn to receive the message without the help of any machines. That way you can have the guru with you always.

IT WILL LAST A LONG TIME

If you get married to depend on someone, that's not a real marriage. Marriage is equal sharing of life. You both go toward the goal together, helping each other. There should be assistance, not dependence. If you depend on the other person and you don't get what you were expecting, it will disturb your marriage.

True marriage means you don't expect anything from the other partner. You marry someone else to give all that you can. That's the end of it. You don't need to expect anything in return, not even love. The true purpose of a marriage is to give, not to ask for anything for yourself. Such a marriage is a spiritual marriage, one that is not bound by material dependency. You are together in spirit. That is what is meant by a marriage made in heaven. And it will last a long time.

27 February

BY YOUR VERY THOUGHT

Your thought, ideas, and energy can be transferred without even seeing or touching a person. By your very thought, you can send your energy and thought forces anywhere you want. Touching or seeing are limited in a way. In touching you are only using your body; in seeing you are limited to the sense of sight. But the flow of energy is not limited to these things; it can travel fast. Thought forces are even more powerful than physical forces.

THEN WHY SHOULD YOU GO TO SURF?

If you are just going to follow nature and get tossed by the waves, then why should you go to surf? The nature of the ocean is to try to dump you. You are going there to learn to surf without getting dumped.

It is the nature of the mind to constantly change. You should learn how to surf on the waves of the mind, rather than being tossed and beaten by them. Always affirm that you are not going to be the slave of the mind; you are going to be the master. Exercise your mastery.

If something terrible comes, you think, "Oh, I can't bear it. I can't stand it another minute." But if you just hold on a little longer, it passes. Then you are so relieved. Good and bad are all a mental matter. Sometimes white clouds come; sometimes black clouds come. Wait a little; everything passes away. Don't give up. When a restless cloud passes, you are peaceful again.

If you give up and run somewhere else, there will be a difficult situation to face there too. Wherever you go, your own mind goes with you. It will create the same problem, maybe in a different way. If you can keep control over the mind, wherever you are will be a heaven. If you do not have that control, even if you are in heaven it will be a hell for you.

29 February

YOU WILL LAUGH AT YOUR OWN DREAM

Question: If we are all essentially the Absolute, why and how did the illusion begin?

Sri Gurudev: Are you asking this question while still under illusion or from an enlightened position? If the question itself comes from illusion, then the answer will be understood with the same illusion. As long as we are not enlightened, we have to accept the illusion. Instead of trying to find out how it came, it's better to work to get out of it. At least you realize that you are in that illusion. You are in darkness. You are sleeping. You are dreaming. When you wake up you will know what a wild dream you had. While you are still dreaming, however much someone says that you are dreaming, you are still going to wrestle with your pillow and cry. As long as you are dreaming, that dream seems very real. As soon as you wake up, everything is clear. When you wake up you will laugh at your own dream, which was nothing but illusion. When you get enlightened, all the whys and hows are automatically answered. Until then no answer will satisfy you.

March

1 March

NOTHING <u>BRINGS</u> YOU JOY

To enjoy life to the fullest, stop wanting anything. If something comes, let it come. If it goes, let it go. Just be contented with what you have. Even if something goes from what you have, it doesn't matter. Accept it. You should feel, "God gives me everything that I need, and God takes away everything that I don't need." Then you will always enjoy what you have or what you lose. Yes. Enjoy the coming. Enjoy the going. Enjoy the profit, enjoy the loss. The only way to enjoy is to just be what you are. You're not going to enjoy by getting things. If you are going to enjoy by getting things, you are going to be depressed by losing things. True joy doesn't come from anywhere. Nothing *brings* you joy. No person *brings* you joy. You yourself are joyful always. So enjoy that. That's what you call enjoyment. Depend on nothing, because nothing from outside can make you joyful.

RESISTANCE IS NECESSARY

We are all searching for the happiness and peace that we once experienced. Now it seems to be missing. Certainly we want to find it the quickest way possible. Unfortunately, it doesn't come that easily. We have to go through many kinds of resistance. Why? Because only by passing through resistance do we become stronger. Resistance is necessary.

A seed needs some sort of resistance. That's why you dig a hole, put the seed in, and cover it up. Then it says, "Oh, you think you are going to stop me here? I'm going to come up!" It pushes through and grows strong.

So don't look for the way of least resistance. No matter how big that resistance is, face the situation. Your own strength, your own mental courage will help you a lot. Once you feel that, "Yes, I can win it!" you will win. Don't say, "Ahhh, I don't know. I'll try." No. With that attitude, you have already lost seventy-five percent of your strength. Be bold. Be strong. "I *will* achieve it. Today or tomorrow I am going to get it." That's very important. You need that will to achieve what you really want in life.

3 March

TO WHICH CATEGORY DO YOU BELONG?

We all have a duty toward our children, our parents, our neighbors, our sisters, our brothers, toward everything with which we come into contact. We have a duty toward the land that brings us food, toward the rain that brings us water, toward nature. We are constantly getting things from nature, and we have to return something in some form to that nature, to God.

This is what the Hindu scriptures call *yagnya*, or sacrifice. What is sacrifice? To give at least a little more than you get. There are several types of people in the world. One group always gets and never gives anything back; they are called thieves. Another group gets a lot and gives a little; they are debtors. The third group gets one hundred percent and gives back one hundred percent; they are fair business people. Whatever you get, you give back. Then you are not a debtor, you are not a thief; you are a fair business person.

There is another group of people. They get something but they give back much more; they are better people.

The final group doesn't get anything; they just give. They give all that they have. They know only giving. They are the best people. So the five categories are: The thief, the debtor, the business person, the better person, and the best or the super person. Out of the five, to which category do you belong?

4 March

SEE GOD'S HAND

If you have complete trust in God, you learn to accept whatever comes to you. There is no demanding in your life because you know, "Whatever I deserve, God is the one who is giving it to me. If I don't deserve something, God is the one who takes it away."

But God won't come personally to take it away. He will say, "Okay, you! Take that away from her." God works through somebody, even without that person's knowing it. You don't have to look at the person and murmur, "How dare she do that to me!" Instead, see God's hand working through every other hand.

5 March

NO BARGAINS

True love knows no bargains. It is one way traffic: giving, giving, giving.

6 March

THE REASON IS TO TEACH US SOME LESSON

Nothing happens without a reason. The reason is to teach us some lesson. There is always a good lesson in whatever happens to us, even in the midst of our losses. I don't mean only in material losses; it's that way even with losses of our near and dear. The whole world is a university, and we are all here learning. Every individual should think, "I am the only student. Everyone and everything are my professors."

How many families have we had? How many fathers, how many mothers, how many wives and husbands, how many children? Don't think this is the only life you have lived. You have had hundreds of lives before, and you will have many more. There is only one unchanging Father and Mother, that Cosmic Consciousness. All others are simply helping you to pass through.

In a way, even our our kith and kin, our own near and dear are educating us to this truth. We should learn to accept and understand that.

SEND OUT THE PRAYERS

Don't think that because you pray, somebody gets healed. No. God is not to be fooled that way. He didn't give someone a problem because you didn't pray. He did it to teach that person a lesson. By praying for someone, you open your heart. You become more compassionate; and of course your prayerful thoughts will reach the person being prayed for. If the person deserves to receive them, he will. Even if that happens, don't think that your prayer literally cured him. Your prayer *helped* him.

Peaceful and healing thought forms spread, and the person who is ready to receive gets healed. That is the power of prayer. Prayers bring powerful thoughts. If the sick person really looks for it and wants it, he or she can use it. You simply make it available. But you cannot force it onto him. If his previous offense was that big, his own destiny might cause him to reject the prayer. Such a person cannot be helped.

Don't think that because you appeal to God, God simply obeys you. That would mean that God doesn't love that person, and will only help him because you prayed. No. You should remember that each one is God's child. God doesn't wait for your prayers in order to take care of His children.

Your duty is simply to send the prayers. If the person for whom you're praying is ready, he or she will receive the prayer. If not, somebody else might get the benefit. That is why we pray for the entire world.

Send out the prayers, broadcast. Whoever tunes in, will receive it.

8 March

THE FINAL STRAW

You cannot say exactly what will open your mind and when it will happen. The real knowledge or wisdom will not dawn slowly. Once you get it, you have it. If you don't get it, you don't have it. The realization doesn't come little by little. Realization is instantaneous. When will it happen? Nobody can tell you. Even a small, trifling thing could do it.

I will tell you a story about a saint named Patinatar. His father was a very rich man who had made a lot of money from shipping and other businesses. The father had seen many saints and sages and had studied a lot, but nothing had opened his mind to the Truth. He repeated his mantra regularly, performed religious rituals, did all the spiritual practices, but wisdom didn't dawn in him. One day he asked his son, Patinatar, to take his ship and go buy some merchandise. Patinatar went to an island and saw the poor people there. He spent all the money, millions of dollars, on helping these people. Patinatar realized that he couldn't go home with an empty ship, so he filled the entire ship with cow dung cakes, which were probably worth a hundred dollars or less. Then he sailed home.

As soon as the boat arrived, some of the boatmen ran to the father and told him, "Your son has gone crazy. He spent all of your money, and all he came back with is cow dung." The father was so upset that he didn't even want to see his son. When Patinatar arrived at the house, his father was not even there to greet him.

Patinatar gave a small package to his mother and said, "Please give this to my father when he comes. I will see you later." With that, he walked out. When the father came home, he asked, "Where is my son?" His wife told him that Patinatar had come and gone, and gave him the package. When the father opened the package, he found a broken sewing needle and a note. The note said, "Even the eye of a broken needle will not come with you on your final journey." As soon as he read those words, he immediately took off his fancy clothes, put on a loin cloth, said goodbye to his house and his businesses, and walked out. Realization had dawned in him. He had heard many hundreds of stories before, he had read volumes, he knew all the philosophy, but nothing had opened his eyes until he saw these few words.

Realization can dawn with the smallest thing. It doesn't have to be a big blow. That trifling thing is what you call the final straw. Wisdom dawns that way. At any moment, anything could be the last straw for you. Then

you are enlightened. Until then, you are still preparing yourself. You are getting ready for that moment.

9 March

DON'T DO IT HALFWAY

If you want to experience the truth that everything happening is the Divine Will, you have to accept it totally. If you sleep, it's the Divine Will that makes you sleep. If you overeat, it's the Divine Will that makes you overeat. If you fall sick, that's Divine Will also. You must accept it *all* as Divine Will.

If you feel that something from outside prompts you to do it, that is Divine Will. You need never feel guilty about it. Something may prompt you from within, and your ego may say, "Do it. Go ahead." If you really feel that everything is Divine Will, even that prompting from your ego comes from the higher source.

You may be directed to save a life; that's Divine Will. Your ego may tell you, "Go and eat a lot of pizza!" If you have the attitude I'm talking about, you will know that this is also Divine Will. Afterward you should not feel guilty, since it was the Divine Will.

Don't do this halfway. Either feel that it is *all* Divine Will or it is all your will.

If you totally trust the Divine Will, it will not bring conflict. Even if your ego prompts you to do something wrong, God will say, "She is completely trusting Me. Her ego is prompting this, but she is doing it in My name. I should stop it." God will take care of your ego for you.

It is easy to talk about, but very hard to practice. Until you achieve that highest surrender, you can think, "Whatever mistake I do is from my weakness. It's my ego that makes me do these things." If everything is nice, "Ah. God must have prompted me to do this. That is why it has come out well." That way you are always safe.

10 March

LAUGH AT IT AND BE BRAVE

Question: I have a vision defect which, with other problems, leads to despair and a feeling that I am only awaiting death. What can I do?

Sri Gurudev: What a pity. Why should you await death? Don't think that seeing with the eyes is the most important thing. Do you think people who can see well are happy just because of that? In a way, you are fortunate. I tell this even to blind people. How many problems are caused by the things people see? The physical senses can be a tremendous distraction. If you have them, take care of them and use them well. If you don't have them, don't worry about it; just forget it. You still have your beautiful mind, your beautiful soul. Many, many people who have limited physical sight, or even no physical sight at all, do great things. You shouldn't be discouraged.

If there is an operation that will help your condition, certainly try it. If there is no possibility of correcting it, it doesn't matter. Accept it as what God wanted you to have. The minute you learn to accept something, it is no longer that troublesome. You can live with anything and everything. Haven't you known of people in worse conditions living happily and usefully? The problem is in the mind. If you just accept it, it becomes very easy, very light.

If you want to feel bad, you have many hundreds of excuses; but if you want to be happy, you can be happy without any of these things. It's useless to worry about them. After all, it's just a body. The so-called limitations should not spoil your joy. Remind yourself: "I'm not the body. I'm not even the mind. I'm the spirit." Laugh at it and be brave.

11 March

A BEAUTIFUL FIELD

If you choose the path of marriage, it is a beautiful field in which to learn the great qualities of sharing and sacrificing. Before you marry, ask yourself, "Can I share my love and my life with someone? Can I dedicate my whole life to that person?"

After marriage your life becomes divided—a little for you, a little for your partner. Then one or two babies come. You share even more with them. You are gradually dividing yourself, sharing your life with many others. You learn how to take care of them; you have more responsibility, and you are tested constantly. In school you are tested. Why? It helps you to find out whether you learned properly or not. It also helps others to know whether you studied well or not. So in family life you also have tests to face. If you don't want to answer the questions and solve the problems there, if you just quit this examination and go somewhere else, eventually you will find an examiner standing in that place too. Wherever you go, you cannot escape from that.

12 March

HE NEVER TAKES SIDES

God is neutral. He never takes sides. You should also be that neutral, that pure. Don't ever discriminate between people. Don't ever look down on anybody. See the same spirit functioning through all the various bodies and minds.

13 March

A PILGRIMAGE

When God wants you to pray to Him, He creates some uncomfortable situation. He makes you run out of gas, or maybe something much worse. That's why we say, "Adversities are blessings in disguise." When we face situations like that, when we face a crisis, we think of God more. At other times we *do* think of Him, but only superficially. It's not really deep. Our prayer becomes sincere and deep only when we have some crisis to make us realize our limitations. "That's all, I can't do any more. Now I leave it to You. I trust You. Please do something." In a way, life itself is a journey toward God. A pilgrimage, in a way. A real pilgrimage is when you go with nothing in the hand, totally depending on God.

14 March

PERFECTION DOESN'T COME OVERNIGHT

Keep in mind that you want to perfect your life; but know that perfection doesn't come overnight. Making mistakes is part of learning to be perfect. So when you make a mistake, don't get upset. Find out the cause for the mistake, what situation caused you to make the mistake. Learn from your mistakes, and then don't repeat them. You are free to make another kind of mistake, but not the same mistake. Every mistake, every failure is a stepping stone for future success.

The problem with so-called perfectionists is that they don't like to accept failure. You *have* to fail. Look at an Olympic champion, a great runner. Did he or she run out of the womb at birth? Did he start life running? No. He couldn't even move his body much. How long did it take for that future champion to be able to stand? To walk? To run? How many times did she fall?

That is the process of learning. Don't be afraid of falling. Let every failure help you to learn a little better for your future success. If you keep that in mind, then you won't get caught in what is called perfectionism.

Everybody learns in this way. In fact, nobody is ever one hundred percent perfect. There will still be a little imperfection. When you have become completely perfect, you won't even be in this world anymore.

15 March

YOU CAN'T FLY LIKE A BIRD

Ultimately the Higher Will is the final authority. In the case of human beings, free will has been given with certain limitations. You are not free to do everything you want. You can't fly like a bird. There are many other such limitations. Your will is limited, but within those limitations you are allowed to do certain things freely. Those things are: to be helpful to other beings, to be serviceful to other beings, and to live a harmonious and useful life. You are free to do that. At the same time, you are also free not to live that way. By your own free will, you will face the result of whatever you do. You are even told what is right and what is wrong, but nobody interferes with your free will.

It's been that way since the very first person. According to the Bible, Adam was asked not to eat the fruit. But God had given him free will, and Adam chose to eat the fruit. Did God stop him? No. That is where your free will comes in. You are free even to do wrong things, but you cannot escape from the guilt of having done something like that. That's why Adam felt guilty.

Was it God's intent to make him feel guilty? No. Through that guilt, God wanted him to learn a lesson. Learning a lesson is more important, so you are allowed to commit the mistake, feel guilty, and from that learn the lesson. Experience is the best teacher. That's why free will is given.

Those who really want to use free will in the right way would choose by their own free will to give themselves into the hands of the Higher Will. With your free will you say, "Lord, You have given me free will. I know it has limitations. I can only do certain things, and if I try to go beyond those limitations Your will comes and stops me. So what is the idea of having my free will? To have fun? It's better not to use my free will because ultimately You are the boss. Your Will is the final one, so I give my free will into Your hands. You gave it to me; now please take it back and do whatever You want." With your own free will you give yourself into the hands of God. We never lose by giving ourselves into those hands. By giving ourselves completely, we gain more of God. We get all of God, if we give our all. Then there is no destiny, and there are no problems.

16 March

THE MEANING OF OM

OM is the sound of the Cosmic Vibration. The entire cosmos vibrates. Every cell vibrates. In fact, the whole universe is nothing but sound vibrations. The basic vibration is a hum, and the sum total of the universal vibration is also a hum. In between, there are fragments. All the words, all the languages, all the various sounds that are created by the human beings or animals or even machines are smaller parts of this cosmic hum. Without that hum, there is nothing. To denote that cosmic hum, there should be a word. OM is the word that comes closest to representing that cosmic hum. The word OM itself is not the hum. It's the name of the hum.

17 March

WHAT WOULD YOUR HANDS DO?

A friend is not necessarily someone to always smile at you and go with you to parties. A real friend should be able to help you in becoming a better person. A friend in need is a friend indeed. What is your need? To maintain your peace, your health and happiness. A friend should be a good aid to that. Often we may find it difficult to travel alone. The path is steep. It is always better to have somebody who can help you, who can hold you and see that you don't slip. We should always look for such friends and, once we find them, we should never lose them.

A real friend will not hesitate to point out your mistakes. Those who do hesitate are just there to exploit you. You are a comfortable person for them to be around, and they can get something from that. So it is for their own benefit that they are keeping their friendship with you. They are afraid of losing it. A real friend will think of your benefit, not of his or her own. If need be, that friend will be ready even to give up his life for you.

In the Thirukkural, Sri Thiruvalluvar describes what friendship is. In South India, where he lived, the men wear *dhotis.* A *dhoti* is a long piece of cloth worn tied around the waist. Imagine that you are wearing a *dhoti* and you are speaking in front of a group of people; and, as you stand there, all of a sudden your *dhoti* slips. What would your hands do? Immediately they would catch it. They wouldn't even wait for a second. That's what you call friendship: the hands that would help you to hold your *dhoti* when it falls. A true friend will not hesitate even for an instant. Immediately he or she will jump in and do what is necessary to help.

When will you know if a person is really a friend or not? Only when you are facing some difficulty.

IT'S SOMETHING BLISSFUL

How can anyone explain that Cosmic Consciousness? It's like trying to measure the sky with a twelve-inch ruler. Our measuring instruments—the mind and the vocabulary—are very, very limited. All we can say is, "It's something blissful."

In that blissful state you always experience joy. You never get disturbed by anything. You never feel any anxiety or worry or fear. In that state of Cosmic Consciousness, there is no fear at all because you see everything as the same: one essence expressed as many. You learn to accept everything as part of the different expressions. In that state there's no friend, there's no enemy; it is all the same.

We often see images of God with one hand raised, the palm facing outward. That is the hand of fearlessness. The other hand will be pointed down, again with the palm outward. What is He telling us? "If you humble yourself and take refuge at my feet, you have nothing to fear."

Attaining the feet of the Lord means attaining God-Consciousness. When you have that God-Consciousness, you know that *everything* is God, no matter what it looks like. Then why should we be afraid of anything? The *Bhagavad Gita* says it beautifully: "Who is a great sage? The one who neither brings fear to anyone, nor is afraid of anyone." Such a person is a person with that supreme, infinite God-Consciousness.

19 March

LOSSES ARE ALWAYS GREAT EYE OPENERS

Question: Very recently, all of my possessions were stolen. What is there to be learned from this experience?

Sri Gurudev: Those things have served you enough; you don't need them anymore. And somebody else probably needed them more than you did. If you still need some of them, you can afford to replace them. God knows that also. But most important of all, you still have yourself. Nobody can steal that.

This kind of experience is God's way of making you renounce your attachments. This is the time to check to see how many things you are attached to. Are you suffering because you lost your possessions? Or are you undisturbed, happy and peaceful?

Life is filled with such tests. But only lucky people will get tested in this way. Without this experience, you might have thought that you were a wonderful yogi because there was nothing to disturb you; everything seemed beautiful. Only when adversities come do you have an opportunity to prove what you have learned.

Losses are always great eye openers. Pleasures never open our eyes. It's only through pain that we learn our weaknesses.

20 March

THEY WILL COME TO YOU MORE

Question: Today's business world is hard and competitive. What would you advise a young person who plans to start a business?

Sri Gurudev: It *is* competitive in the business world; and unfortunately or fortunately all the gimmicks seem to be paying off. A lot of money is made by gimmicks, by adulterations and things like that. By false advertising. So it's very hard to have a straight business and compete with those businesses. But if people come to realize that you are running an honest business, certainly they will come to you more. You will never have difficulty in getting enough customers. After some time the truth comes out. Business should be done with service in mind. Think of the benefit of the buyers. Your duty is to give them the right product or service at the right price with a marginal profit for you. You have to continue your business, so your profit can be a little above your overhead expenses to allow for rainy seasons. And business is not always the same. So you have every right to have a little profit; but not too much. Sell as if you were the buyer.

21 March

HONEST WANT IS PRAYER

By sincere prayer you put yourself in a receptive mood. You become a good receiver. You tune your heart radio. Prayer is a form of tuning. Once you tune your heart through prayer, you get all the cosmic things. Whatever you pray for, you get. Pray for peace, you are tuning your radio to the peace station. Pray for beauty, you tune your radio to the beauty station.

More things are wrought by prayer than the world dreams of. We don't know the power of prayers. Don't we say, "You want it, you got it!" It is literally true; if you really want it sincerely, you get it.

Real want, sincere want, honest want is prayer. Through that sincere prayer, you tune your heart to God.

22 March

THE FIRST DUTY

A spiritual seeker's first duty is to have good control over the tongue. Without control of the tongue we can forget about spirituality. Control in both ways: eating and talking. All the senses are controlled if the tongue is controlled.

23 March

YOU WILL ONLY SEE BEAUTY

Judging others is an act of the ego; it's a kind of arrogance. It means that you think you're a great person and all the others are fools. Others may have a problem, but to judge them means that *you* have at least one kind of problem yourself, the problem of constantly criticizing people. You are actually no different from them. Before you see a mote in their eyes, see the beam in your own eye.

The vulture flies so high, higher than many birds. It can see far and wide. But where will its eyes be? On a dead and decayed body somewhere. It soars beautifully and high; but it doesn't cast its eyes on good, holy things, only on decayed matter. An ordinary fly looks for filthy matter to sit on, while a honeybee will fly past many other things to look for even a little bit of nectar on a flower.

You see certain things in others because you have the eye to see it. If you have a beautiful eye, you will see only beauty. Know that everyone has some sort of weakness. A person who doesn't have any weakness at all won't even be on this earth.

Don't have the kind of eye that finds faults in others. Be humble and correct your own problems.

24 March

DO A DIRTY JOB

How do we learn humility? Only by putting ourselves in the field and doing honest, hard work. Don't just sit and meditate or stand on your head for an hour and a half at a time. Your ego will be boosted if you stand on your head that long. It is when you put your hand in the mud and mire and do a dirty job that you learn to be humble. Humility is a great virtue. It shows the purity of the mind.

25 March

SOMETIMES WE LOSE OUR STRENGTH

Question: One of my employees stole an item from one of our customers. I have given him a second chance, but others are expressing a feeling of mistrust in him. What should I do?

Sri Gurudev: See if that employee is ready to openly apologize and repent for what he has done. It would probably be best for him to do it in front of the rest of the employees, not just the employer. People *do* make mistakes. Sometimes in a weak moment we lose our strength and do something that's not right. The minute you realize that you have done something wrong, you should not hesitate to come and say openly, "Yes, I made a mistake. I was weak. I'm sorry for it and I will try my best not to repeat that. Please keep an eye on me and help me." If you are really interested in changing for the better, you should seek the help of others. This employee should come forward and openly apologize and ask for help. If that is done, I think not only the employer, but the other employees also will feel sympathetic and compassionate toward him and agree to have him continue in that job.

If I were the employer, and if I had an employee like that, that's what I would do. To err is human. Even the employer might have done the same thing at one time or another. We all make mistakes. It's always better to forgive and forget, and not to always treat the person as a liar or a thief. We should give more and more and more chances for people to grow.

26 March

SINCE THEN I AM NEVER ALONE

Question: There are times when I feel very deep loneliness that no friend, family member or lover can seem to satisfy. Do you ever get lonely like that?

Sri Gurudev: Long ago I *used* to feel lonely until I realized that there is a Lover who is always in me, with me, next to me, closer than my heart. That is God, or the Self. Since then, I have found that I am never alone.

If you depend on anything or anybody outside you to be a companion, it is impossible to have that companion always with you. Even if another person wants to be with you always, he or she cannot. We come alone, and we go alone. Don't depend on outside company. Even as you are coming and going, there is always another there—your own spirit, your own Self, or the God within you. He is in you, outside of you, in front of you and behind you, to the right, to the left, above and below. The moment you realize that, you will never feel lonely. Unfortunately we seem to be depending on outside things and people for company. The outside company is fine, but don't *depend* on it. Be independent of everything. If it comes, fine. If it goes, wonderful.

Just because I say, "Don't depend on that," you don't have to reject something if it comes to you. Let it come whenever it wants, and let it go whenever it chooses. Give everything that freedom. The minute you try to cling to something or someone and say, "I want to keep you with me always," you are creating big trouble. Nobody can be with you always except that God in you.

Just because you hear it, it's not going to happen overnight. You have to contemplate on it. Think of the pros and cons of your depending on other things and other people for your happiness. The more you think about it, the more you will realize, "Yes, I cannot depend on anything. I can't even depend on the body. I'm keeping it for now, but every day it is little by little getting older. Beauty isn't permanent. Money isn't permanent. Friends aren't permanent. Name isn't permanent. Fame isn't permanent."

See if you can name anything that is permanent other than God.

27 March

WHERE SHOULD IT BEGIN?

Mantrams have great power. Modern science has proven it. With sound vibration, you can make or break. You can heal, or you can produce disease. You can make somebody laugh, you can make somebody cry with your sound. You can turn a human being into an animal who will go out and fight. You can pacify a baby. You can enchant a cobra. You can get more milk from your cow with a little music. Plants grow with nice music. It's true, and it's all being proved nowadays.

So your mantra repetition is nothing different. Certain mantrams can easily cure all your problems, physical and mental. Even repeating, "OM *Shanthi,* OM *Shanthi,* OM *Shanthi.*" *Shanthi* means peace, but it also has that peaceful vibration. It's very powerful. When you fill your system with that vitality, with that health and happiness, you become contagious. Fill yourself up to the brim with health and let it overflow. Just by your mere presence, you will bring health to others. You can pass it on to others. You will constantly emit that vibration. That will be the beginning of world health. Where should it begin? Right with you.

TUNE TO GOD'S FREQUENCY

The best way to clean your system is to use sound. Simply choose any holy name you like, and keep repeating it. Let your body vibrate with that frequency. In the beginning you have to concentrate on that vibration within you. But as you continue, every cell in your body will begin to repeat your mantram or your prayer; then the whole system, the whole personality, body, mind, everything will vibrate on that wavelength. The holy word is like a radio wave.

When a mantram is given to you, you tune your personality to a particular frequency. It's just like tuning a radio. The cosmic music that comes from God is always being transmitted; God never stops transmitting all the beautiful things. Some simply don't tune their heart radios to the proper frequency. Instead, they tune it to the wrong frequency and get atmospheric disturbance.

With practice, you'll be able to tune your heart radio. You will become a good receiver. Only then is the proper communication possible. Communication brings communion. Real communion is possible only when you tune your entire personality to God's frequency.

29 March

A TEEPEE ON MARS

The mind is restless; it is always looking for a change. That is the nature of the mind. It can never be satisfied. It might rebel and want you to go live in a teepee in the mountains. After a while it won't be happy with your teepee on the mountaintop; it will think that only putting a teepee in the valley will make you happy. Once you are in the valley, it will want a teepee on Mars. There is no limit for the mind's restlessness.

You have to educate the mind. Ask it, "Why do you want to go to the mountain?" "To find peace there." "Why do you want to come down?" "I am tired of that and want to be with people."

What does it all mean? That you are trying to borrow happiness from outside. Once you realize that peace and joy are always within you, you will be happy no matter where you are. Whether you are in the valley or in the mountains, it is the same thing. Whether you are on the earth or on Mars, it is the same thing.

Wherever you are, you should have a purpose. Go to the mountain for a purpose; come down for a purpose. And don't let that purpose be a selfish one. The purpose should be for the benefit of others, for service to humanity.

30 March

ONE CATCHWORD

Keep at least one catchword for your life. It can be anything that will remind you always of the highest truth. It need not be the same word for everyone. If there is some inspiring phrase or word that particularly strikes you, that's your catchword. In any situation where you feel a little shaky, think of that catchword. It will immediately elevate you and lift you above the problem.

31 March

EVERYTHING GOES SMOOTHLY

Question: How can I know if I am following the Will of God when I make a decision?

Sri Gurudev: You will find out very soon. It won't take very long. If it is the Will of God, everything will go smoothly. If it is your egoistic will, you'll get the blow right away. God's Will is always for the benefit of everybody, including you. Your egoistic thought is selfish; it wants your benefit first. The ego always wants something for itself.

April

1 April

OUR LIVES WILL BE SUPER PEACEFUL

If you totally surrender yourself into the hands of God, you will feel: "God, I didn't plan to come here. You sent me here. You have a purpose. I don't know what that purpose is. If I could ask You for anything, it would be this: 'Let me always remember that You are working through me. I am not responsible for any of these things. Please let me not forget this.'"

If this is our prayer, our lives will be super, super peaceful. If you have that faith, His power will make you think, make you do. Even the impulse to act comes from Him. When you become a good instrument, the ideas are dropped in. They come and prompt you, "Okay now, go ahead, do this." Your job is to simply allow it to happen.

2 April

LOVE EVEN THE MOSQUITOES THAT BITE YOU

Universal love means to see the same Self in everything. Unlimited, unconditional love is universal. If you have universal love, there is not even a single thing you dislike. You love everything, even the mosquitoes that bite you. You don't dislike them; you simply say, "Well, mosquito, that is the purpose for which you were created. You are doing your job in biting me. I am doing my job and saying, 'Please get out.'" You don't stop loving the mosquito. But loving the mosquito doesn't mean allowing it to bite you. Often people think, "Because I love that mosquito, I cannot chase it away." That's not so. You can *love* the poison, but you don't have to *swallow* it.

3 April

GOD'S CLUB

If you want to become a member of God's club, get all the qualifications needed to become a member. Only a rich person can go to the rich people's club. Only a spiritual person can go to the spiritual people's club.

If you want God, become God soon. Until you become God, you will never understand what God is. Have you ever seen God sick and dirty and eating all the wrong things? No. So you should eat what God eats. God's altar is neat and tidy, clean, absolutely pure, not even a speck of dust. But you go to your room and it's a junkyard. And you want God. Let your very life reflect God's purity. Your place, your body and your mind should be that pure, as pure as God; then you will see God.

"Blessed are the pure in heart, they shall see God." That means you have to raise yourself to that caliber. You should be that pure. Otherwise, just crying for God is not going to help you much. Think, why is it you are not getting God, you are not experiencing God? What prevents you? Eliminate all these things. Purify yourself. That's what you call *tapasya* or austerity. Fire is the best purifier. There's nothing greater than fire to burn out all the dust, all the junk. Burn yourself in the fire of the holy name. Your own mantram is a fire. Kindle it up. Let it blaze in you. Burn out all your sins and toxins. And the moment you come to the same level of purity, I don't have to tell you what will happen to you.

4 April

PUT YOURSELF IN HIS PLACE

Question: Often I see others making a mistake, and would like to suggest another way of handling things. How can I do it without making the other person react defensively?

Sri Gurudev: Do it in a gentle way. The reason the other person becomes defensive is that you are immediately putting blame on him or her. He doesn't want to accept that. Even if your observation is correct, he may not be able to accept it. His ego won't allow it; so it puts a block there. That's defense.

If you really want to help the person, first know his or her nature. Will he really accept and appreciate your advice? If you are a little doubtful but you still want to say something, just cook up a different way of presenting it. Say, "You know, I had the same problem the other day, and I had two ways to act. Thank God I went this way. If I had done it the other way I would certainly have gotten into trouble. Luckily I chose this one. I'm just sharing this with you. If you find it helpful, take it." Put yourself in the other person's place. There is a gentle way of saying it.

If you put things like this, he or she won't immediately feel defensive. Sometimes if you state the plain truth in plain language, you hurt the other person, and you get hurt as well. We have to learn how to communicate.

YOU SHOULD KNOW HOW TO COMMUNICATE

Once upon a time there lived a king who really wanted a son. After many, many years his wife at last gave birth to a boy. The king was joyous. Immediately he called all the astrologers to learn his son's future. Many great astrologers came to study the boy's horoscope. Each one studied the charts. The signs were quite clear. "Sir," the astrologers said, "your son is not a good child. Because of him you will die by the time he reaches the age of ten. In a way, he has come to kill you."

The king was furious. "You devils! You don't even know how to cast a horoscope. Throw them all in jail."

One day an astrologer from far away came to the kingdom. The king immediately asked him to look at his son's chart. The astrologer studied the horoscope carefully and said, "I have never seen a horoscope like this! It's a very strong horoscope. Your son will live a long life and will be a great king. He will live for one hundred years after you have died." This astrologer was a very clever man; he read the same chart as the others, but he presented the information in a completely different way.

The king was so happy. "Shower this man with gifts. He is a great astrologer. If there is anything you want, sir, just ask me."

"Well," the astrologer said, "There is just one request."

"Of course. What is it?"

"Please release those other poor astrologers from the prison. Their only crime was not being very smart. They know how to calculate, but they don't know how to communicate." Because of this one man all the others were set free.

Mere education is not enough. You should know how to deal with people, how to communicate, how to live harmoniously with others. That is a great lesson that cannot be learned from books alone. Learn to live harmoniously. That is where the real joy and peace lie.

6 April

YOU DON'T HAVE TO BE AFRAID OF ANYTHING

Have complete faith. Don't even go near fear. Remember: If anything has to happen, it will happen. Think, "All right, let it happen. I am bold! What's the use of being afraid of it? I'm not going to be able to stop anything that is meant to happen."

If you really have faith, you don't have to be afraid of anything. That doesn't mean that you should not be careful. Be careful, but don't be afraid.

7 April

THE SECRET

As you think, so you become. If you always think of breaks, you will break. Just enjoy the work. Real joy comes when you work for others and not for yourself. When you work for yourself, you develop anxiety, you develop worry and fear. When you work for others there is joy.

That is karma yoga, selfless service. If you really want to enjoy your work, this is the only way. Work for others or work for God, in the name of God and His creation. Just put yourself out of the picture. "I am not doing anything for myself. I don't have to; I don't want to. I am here to serve others." You take care of them. If the others need your service, it's their business to take care of *you*. You don't have to worry about taking care of yourself.

Remember: If you decide to take care of yourself, you are the only person to take care of you. If you let others take care of you, so many will do that.

That's the secret. Don't worry about taking care of yourself. Just think of others; then you will be taken care of.

8 April

AN OUNCE OF FAITH

Faith and fear don't go together. If you have faith, there is *nothing* to be afraid of. "God is the one who sent me; God is the one who is keeping me alive; God is the one who is doing everything to me. Whatever I need, God is going to give me. If I don't need something, He won't give it to me. Even if I cry, He won't give it to me if it's not needed. Why? Because it may not be good for me." So just have faith. An ounce of faith will make you super happy.

IF YOU WANT TO, YOU CAN DO IT

When you want to cultivate something, you have to look for a little culture. The same is true if you want to cultivate faith. Think of all the sayings, all the great teachings and apply them in your life. Before a farmer cultivates, what does he do? He first prepares the soil by taking out all the stones and twigs, leveling the ground, loosening the soil, putting in some manure, aerating it, and then planting some good seed.

In our own lives, we have to go through a similar preparation. The seeds are the good thoughts from the scriptures and the great sages and saints. Put them in and nurture them. Let them grow in your life.

Cultivation is not that easy. It takes effort; but certainly if you want to, you can do it. To achieve the small things in life, you have to work very hard; but to achieve the spiritual goals, everything is done once you have that faith.

When a person is trying to cultivate faith, there will be hundreds of things to come and disturb it. There will be tests. Immediately things will come to create doubt in your life. Somebody will say, "God, Enlightenment—why worry about all that? Enjoy life. You are missing so many nice things by concentrating on the spiritual life."

It is not just in this age. For millions of years the same thing has happened. There are so many temptations to forget about spirituality. "Free me from temptation," is one of the important prayers. "Take me to the real pasture where I can graze. Do not take me into areas where I will be distracted." Have sincere, heartfelt prayer. It is not easy to build faith. Keep praying, "God, please help me. Let me see the Truth always."

THEN YOU TRY TO SHAKE THE POST

Even your spiritual practices are based on faith. If you didn't have faith, you wouldn't even be practicing. Everything requires faith. That is why the scriptures say that if you have faith the size of a mustard seed, you can move mountains.

Strong conviction is faith. If you have conviction, it is easy to accomplish what you set out to do. But before you even begin, you must be convinced. Otherwise you will just think, "Oh, okay, I'll *try* to do it." Don't think that way. Your thought should be, "This is what I want, no matter what happens. All the rest is nothing. I won't stop until I get it! This is the most important thing in my life."

Tests will come to see if you are really strong in your faith. Do you know how to install a flag post or a telephone post in the ground? You dig a hole and put the post in; but you don't just leave it at that. You put stones all around and hammer it to make it strong. You hammer the ground all around, and then you try to shake the post. If it shakes, you hammer again. As long as it keeps shaking, you keep on hammering. When do you stop hammering? When it stops shaking.

Life is like that. As long as you are shaking, you'll be hammered. It's true. God is trying to make you steady, and unless that hammering occurs you cannot be strong and steady. So don't be afraid to face the hammering.

THE HIGHEST FORM OF FAITH

If you have absolute faith you don't have to do anything. You will accept everything—even if you sometimes feel foolish. "I am foolish? Well, God made me that way. I don't know why He did that, but He must have had some reason for it. If He doesn't want me to be foolish anymore then He will take care of it."

That is the highest form of faith. If you can't easily develop that kind of faith, your prayer can be, "God, let me have faith in You. Let me know that You are doing everything for me. You are taking care of me. Please give me a mind that can always remember this truth. Sometimes I forget that; I know You are testing me then. Even when I forget, you are the culprit who made that happen! Still I can't help asking for You not to make me forget."

IT'S ALL FOR GOOD

Once upon a time there was a king who had a wonderful, wise minister. The minister was very loyal and devoted to the king, and the king never left the palace without the minister at his side.

One day as the monarch was cutting a piece of fruit, he accidentally cut his finger. As it was being treated, he asked the minister why this had happened. "I was very careful," he explained, "but the knife just seemed to slip all by itself." The minister looked at him and gently said, "Don't worry, raja. It's all for good."

The king became furious. "What kind of philosophy is this? I have cut my finger. The blood is pouring. Yet you stand there calmly and say, 'It's all for good.' If that is as much as you care about me, I don't want you around anymore." He called the guards and told them to take the minister to jail. The minister quietly submitted. As he was being taken away, he simply said, "Fine. This also is for good."

Several days later, the king decided to go hunting. He went far into the forest with a large group of companions. Suddenly he started chasing a beautiful deer. Of course he had the fastest horse, and he soon left the others far behind. Still, the deer managed to escape. When the king realized how far he had gone, it was too late. He was very deep into the jungle and was lost.

Fortunately the raja had been on many adventures, and he stayed calm. He was very tired and thirsty. Nearby there was a big, green tree with a small brook running past it. He drank his fill, then leaned against the tree and fell asleep.

In a little while, a rustling sound woke the king. He slowly opened his eyes. What he saw made him freeze. A huge lion was standing right next to him, sniffing him all over. He didn't know what to do so he just stayed still and watched the lion. All of a sudden, as the lion was sniffing one of the king's hands, it snorted and ran away.

The king was amazed at his good fortune. He leaped up and began shouting for his companions, who eventually found him. "Listen," he told them. "A lion came while I was sleeping. He was huge and ferocious-looking. He was all ready to eat me, but something mysteriously happened. All of sudden the lion just left."

"That's wonderful!" they exclaimed; but none of them could explain what had happened. When they returned to the palace the king had the minister brought from the jail. He told the story in every detail. The minister simply said, "It's all for good, Maharaja."

"What do you mean all for good? That doesn't explain why the lion just went away without even biting me. What is the explanation?"

"Maharaja, the lion is the king of the beasts, just as you are the king of the people. When somebody offers you a fruit, it should be a clean, wholesome fruit. The minute the lion smelled the cut finger, it knew that you were not whole, not fit. As the king of beasts, it didn't want to eat you. So you see, raja, the cut finger saved your life. Now do you understand that it's all for good?

"As for my imprisonment, you know that ordinarily we are never separated. Surely I would have been with you on the hunt and would have raced after you through the jungle. We would have both been sleeping under the tree when the lion arrived. He would still have rejected you, but would have swallowed me. Because you had put me in jail, my life was saved."

It is not often easy to see the good in adversity when it occurs. When you find yourself in pain, remember this story of the king and his minister. The benefit may not make itself clear until much later, but it is there. Have faith in the positive outcome. Tell yourself, "It's all for good." It's like a mantram in a way. You can repeat it again and again to give you courage.

13 April

YOU POUR WATER AT THE ROOT OF THE TREE

If you think in terms of how much benefit we get just by being here on the surface of the earth, how much we get from the nature, how much we get from people, how much we get from association, we receive constantly. Good thoughts, good food, good air, good rain. Even the smile from a baby is a gift. When you enjoy the smile of a baby, you are getting something from that baby. And you have to return it; although not necessarily to the same baby. You don't have to give it back at the same place. For example, if you get a nice fruit from the top of a tree, you don't have to go and pour water on the top of the tree. You pour water at the root of the tree. If you pour at the root you get the fruit at the top. In the same way, if you get a smile from a baby, do something to help a poor person somewhere on the road, or a sick person. Somebody who needs a little help. That will balance it out. You got a smile from the baby, and you paid it back by helping that other person. You don't have to give it directly to the baby. We are constantly receiving. Every one of us should think, "How much am I receiving, and how much am I returning?"

DEVELOP THE WILL

Why do people do bad things if they already know what is right and what is wrong? Because of lack of will. We know what is wrong but we don't have the will power to stay away from that. How can one develop the will? By discipline and by regular practice. You develop that will by doing little, little, little things. Don't start with a big job that you cannot easily do; if you fail, you will lose confidence. Accomplishing small things will improve your self-confidence. You will be happy, "Oh, I did it." Then one day, even the biggest thing will be the easiest thing for you.

Will means application of the mind. Training the mind. Making the mind work in a positive way. It's achieved slowly, slowly, slowly, slowly. It's easy to say, "Oh, I'm not made for that. It's too much for me. Not everyone can do that." Such excuses are self-delusion. Without will, we cannot achieve anything.

15 April

YOUR FAITH IN JESUS WASHED YOUR KARMA

Question: Is it proper to say that Jesus took the karma of man upon Himself? Is this the same as other masters' assuming the karma of their disciples?

Sri Gurudev: The masters or prophets or sages do not take away your karma. They can, but normally they don't. Instead, they give you the strength to face your karma and purge it out. It's not right for someone to take away your karma. You are the cause of your karma. You sowed it, and you have to reap it. What you conceived another cannot deliver.

If you really believe the Bible and if you think, "Yes, Jesus took my karma the day I accepted him in my life," then why should you even worry about it? That means you have some doubt. Why? Because it's not that easy. The impure mind will not even allow you to accept the truth. But if you really feel, "Yes, he took my karma and I am completely free from it," then you are free. That does not mean that he took your karma away. How did you get yourself free from karma? By faith. Your faith in Jesus washed your karma. He himself said that, did he not? "Your faith has saved you, your faith has made you whole." If you don't have faith, even Jesus cannot do that, and would not do that.

And why can't you have that faith? Because your own mind is still unclean. It won't harbor that kind of faith. Though you want to have the faith, you are not yet ready. That's why it is said, "Blessed are the pure in heart, they shall see God." Even to have that kind of faith, you should have that kind of perfect purity.

16 April

THE RIGHT THING

How do you know if what you decide to do is the right thing? It's very simple. The right thing will not affect your health and happiness. That's all. Anything that would affect your physical and mental peace, your health and happiness, is wrong. Anything. This might bring another question: "Suppose I want to help somebody who is troubled and that affects me. Should I do it or not?" If you are joyfully serving someone, even going through some pain doesn't affect you. You are still happy; you are simply using a little of your energy to help someone. You can't call that unhappiness.

Sometimes when you help somebody, you feel depressed. Why is that? It is because you had expectations. "I am helping that person. The person should accept my help and get the benefit." When you don't see that person getting the benefit you expected, you get upset. That means it's not a selfless act, it's a selfish act. "I did something and I want a result."

That doesn't mean there shouldn't be positive thoughts behind your actions. Certainly send your prayers, think about the welfare of the person. The difference is this: you want him to be happy of course, but you don't *demand* it. You are not attached to the outcome; you leave that up to God.

In simple words, I would say an action without any selfish expectation whatsoever is a right action. Such an act will never disturb your mind or body.

17 April

STICK TO IT

If you make a vow, no matter what it is, stick to it. Sticking to it is a very difficult thing to do. You will have to face a lot of tests, but be persistent. The ability to persevere will prove that you are the master of your own mind.

18 April

IF YOU SAY "OKAY," LET IT HAPPEN

Don't waste your time in thinking about the past or worrying about the future. Some of the astrologers might be a little unhappy with me for saying that. They have a job to do; fine, let them do it. They are also needed. But don't get caught up in these things. You can rise above your planets. Don't get attached to thinking, "What is your sign? I am an Aquarius. Are you a Taurus? A Capricorn?" You are not any of that. You are the pure Self. Your body and mind have limitations, it is true; but you can rise above them.

It really doesn't help much to know the future. If God had wanted you to know your future, it would have been easy for Him to leave the door open. He knew that it would not be beneficial for you, so He shut the door. It's the same for the past; it's better if you don't remember all the past lives. If you remembered it all, you would still have hundreds of enemies. You might forget all your friends, but you will remember your enemies. Isn't it better to forget them?

Let's not waste time on all these things. Think of the golden present. Enjoy the present. You might still ask, "Don't you think I should at least plan a little bit for my immediate future?" All right, make your plans; but remember: after you make your plans, submit it to Him. "Lord, if You say 'Okay,' let it happen. If not, I won't worry."

19 April

THE BIGGEST MIRACLE

Siddhis or powers can come with spiritual practice. But remember, they are the worst impediments. Who would want a *siddhi?* Your ego. "I want to do this. I want to get that. I want to have name, fame. I want to show my superiority. I want to perform miracles."

The biggest miracle is to become humble. Spiritual growth comes only when you humble your ego. *Siddhis* will never humble your ego.

20 April

NOTHING IS IMPOSSIBLE FOR THE MIND

Nature never discriminates. It has made the same knowledge equally available to everyone. When the mind is calm and clean it can get all the ideas. Nothing is impossible for the mind. If it is completely free from any selfishness, it is always clean and calm, always serene. In such a mind knowledge dawns by itself.

21 April

SHE SHUFFLES THE CARDS

Question: If someone prays for something that feels good and seems right but it doesn't happen, should the person just forget it, or keep praying?

Sri Gurudev: Strictly speaking, your prayer should not be for getting something. It should not be a sort of, "I pray, You give." That does not mean that you should not ask anything of God. You can ask, but don't demand. Say, "Lord, I don't know what's best. I might even be asking for the wrong thing. So if it is Your Will, if You think it's good for me, then please give it to me."

We are nothing but puppets. The force that we call the Cosmic Mother functions through you, through me, through everything—even a speck of dust, or an atom. We say that, but it's not enough. We have to feel it. If we just have that feeling, then whatever we do will become spiritual practice because *we* are not doing it. If someone else does something to you, you should say, "Oh, whatever Mother is doing is Mother's business. She shuffles the cards." Then who is your friend, who is your enemy? We are all one and the same motivated by that power. If you want to pray, say a prayer to God to help you to remember this truth.

In praying for others, we should feel, "Mother, You are putting a desire in my mind to pray for another, so I am praying." Even the idea to pray for someone comes from that Cosmic Source. Otherwise, how could you pray? The good feelings to wish others well comes from that Mother. The power to pray comes from that Mother. The words to pray come from that Mother. The thought has come from the Mother. Even the energy with which you pray comes from that Mother. How can you say, "I am praying for that," as if the Mother were waiting for your prayer to cure that person? As if that person would be doomed without your prayer. That's another subtle form of ego.

22 April

WHAT ELSE DO YOU WANT?

Our understanding is really very, very limited. Still we try to understand why God is doing this and that. It is not possible. For a long time I had this saying on my stationery: "It's all Your Name. It's all Your Form. It's all Your Deed. And it's all for good." Since childhood I believed that, and I have never regretted having that belief. It is that knowledge which keeps me peaceful; I never get upset over anything because it's all for good.

Maybe you will say, "Oh, that's an easy way of escaping;" but all I get is peace. That is something more precious to me than everything in the world. You may call it escapism or blind faith. Whatever it is, I am retaining my peace. That's what I want. Because of that peace, I am always joyful and happy. I don't need to worry about anything. If you have peace and joy, what else do you want?

23 April

IT IS THE ATTITUDE

Who is the real slave? It's not just a person who is purchased by another. If you buy a person and let him work for you, you call him a slave, is it not so? In that sense everyone who works for money is a slave: "Monthly I give you this much money; you work for me." Everybody who works for a reward is a slave, no matter how high his or her position. It is the attitude that makes a real slave. Even the people we normally think of as slaves are actually free people if they have the right understanding. The Self belongs to no one but you; and no matter what happens on the physical level, you are eternally free.

So remember: If you are working because of attachment to a reward, you are a slave. Don't do it. Do your work well; have joy in what you do, but don't look for the fruits of your action. Don't be careless, but do be carefree. Then you are always your own master.

24 April

WELCOME THE DISTURBANCE

Question: You often say, "Don't do anything that would disturb your peace." If someone has an irrational fear, should he or she try to get over it by doing the feared thing, even though this might disturb the person's peace?

Sri Gurudev: In this situation you are consciously trying to get over a phobia. At first, facing it will cause a disturbance; but you should welcome that kind of disturbance. Why? Because the phobia is disturbing you all the time, and this other disturbance is purposely created by you in order to make you well. You are getting some pain in order to get a real gain. If you understand that you are doing it for ultimate benefit, the temporary disturbance of your peace is not going to affect you. The ultimate motive is more important.

Though on the surface you might seem to be getting more disturbed for a short time, within yourself you feel happy about it. There's nothing wrong with getting disturbed in such a way for a good cause.

THOUGHT FORCES ARE VERY POWERFUL

As you send your prayers to a sick person, you can think, "Get well;" but you are not asking God to make the person well. You are simply sending your good thoughts to the one in need. Thought forces are very powerful. They will go and help the person. Your good thoughts, your wishful thinking, will travel to his or her heart.

You can use any words that are meaningful to you. We often use the *Maha Mritunjaya Mantram*. It isn't even asking for someone to be healed; rather it says, "Let him rise above these mortal limitations." It's a good, positive thought you are sending. That way he or she is benefited by your good thoughts, and you are also benefited because you are showing your love. The more you show love and concern to other people, the purer your heart becomes.

26 April

NICE, SOOTHING STORIES

The parents should make the children forget their worries by telling them some nice, soothing stories—something with which they can go to sleep, something that will help them have peaceful dreams. That's what bedtime stories are for, so that the children won't have anything disturbing in their minds.

The stories should be something like this: "Slowly the child gave herself into the hands of God. God put her on His lap. He gently rocked the child and sang a beautiful song. Softly He said, 'Sleep, baby. Sleep, sleep, sleep.' The baby was soon sleeping, and..." It should be a soft, sweet story. The child will imagine that there is a baby resting in God's arms, and God is putting the baby to sleep. He will listen to that story, and when the baby in the story falls asleep, your child will fall asleep too.

27 April

THE CHILD WILL UNDERSTAND YOU

There is a beautiful Tamil lullaby: "Oh my beautiful baby, I call you my baby. I don't know who you are and who I am. I don't know what this relationship is. Where did you come from? Where are you going to go? It happens that we are together. You are my baby, I am your mother; so let's do our job well. You do your job, I'll do my job. You have done it today, you are sleeping today."

In that simple lullaby there is a great spiritual philosophy. "You are pure, you are absolutely clean, you are not tainted by anything. You are that Self. All the rest is just illusion." You might wonder if the child can understand. Simply say it; the child will understand you. The child understands better than many of us. When we can't understand the child, we think the child cannot understand us. Even when the child is in the womb, we can educate it in this way. So instead of simply making all kinds of funny sounds, "Rockabye baby in the treetops," sing a beautiful peace chant: "*Hari* OM" or "OM *Shanthi.*" Let all the babies sleep listening to "OM *Shanthi.*"

28 April

YOU ARE MAKING IT SHINE MORE

Once two children were talking to each other. One child said, "If you show me where God is, I'll give you an apple." The other child looked around and said, "I'll give you *two* apples if you show me where God is not!"

God as holy vibration is everywhere. It is not that you are filling a place with that holy vibration; you are making it express, making it shine more. Imagine a plain stone. Keep rubbing it and it will begin to shine. It will reflect light. If you just leave it crude, it won't reflect the light. By polishing it more, you make it express what was always there.

There are holy vibrations in every place, but it is in our hands to make it a holy place. Sometimes, even if it is a holy place, if we don't reinforce that sanctity, the place will slowly lose its expression of holiness. If you begin to do business or carry on worldly matters there, eventually that high vibration will no longer shine forth. The vibration is to be brought out and expanded. It is the people who come with good intentions and do the spiritual practices who bring out the holy vibrations already existing in a place. In essence, it is the people coming to worship who make it holy.

Some places are holy even before people come to worship there. That is due to the birth of a saint or an event in the life of a saint that took place there. Many holy places are the spots where the bodies of saints are buried. Because their entire personality vibrates with that holy vibration, their bodies are not cremated. Instead, the body is buried so that everything the saint used or touched—including the body—will be there to keep on emitting that holiness. It is because of the presence of the saint that the place manifests that vibration.

29 April

HOLY OBJECTS

Question: If one has a holy object from a saintly person, will that object keep the holy vibration forever?

Sri Gurudev: It depends upon how you keep it. If you keep it in the proper way, in the proper place, without polluting it, it will express that holiness forever. If you just leave it casually somewhere and don't treat it properly, slowly it will lose its energy. All those objects are charged, knowingly or unknowingly, by the touch or use of the holy people. Relics and other items *do* have these vibrations. As long as they are kept with reverence and respect, they will emit more and more vibrations.

30 April

THAT'S YOUR TEST

When you make a vow or a decision, don't expect it to go smoothly. If everything goes smoothly, where is the test to prove that you will stick to that vow? You should even be concerned if no tests come.

If you vow not to eat sweets, very soon someone will offer you the most tempting and unusual treat. If you vow to wake up every morning at 4:30 for meditation, suddenly you will feel so tired. You will only want to sleep.

If you vow to treat your spouse as God, probably at first he or she will look just like a god to you. Maybe for a few days he will act like God also. Then all of a sudden, that same God will turn into something terrible! Even then, don't waver in your vow; continue to think of him or her as God. That's your test. If you pass the test, the situation has become a great instrument for your spiritual growth.

May

1 May

THE SIGN OF A HEALTHY PERSON

What is the sign of a healthy person? Such a person is happy anywhere. He or she is relaxed everywhere—always at ease and in peace, within and without. Even in hell, such a person will be at ease. A healthy person hates no one, dislikes nothing. Total love, universal love emanates from within. There is no tension anywhere, no stress or friction. These are the signs of real health.

A person who is healthy doesn't hurt anyone. He or she is not afraid of anyone. Not only is he unafraid, but he sees that others are not afraid of him. The "others" include animals, plants, everything. A healthy person emits always and only a loving and pure vibration.

A really healthy person takes everything in life as a game. Whether we win or lose, it's still a game. Often people forget that. In a way, I feel that losing is a better game. Why? If you lose, you allow the other person to win. When the other person wins, what do you see? A winning face. When you win and the other fellow loses, what do you see? A losing face. There is great joy in losing and making the other person win and have a happy face. Who will be the happiest person? The one who brings happiness to others. That means our minds should be well balanced under all conditions. That is yoga.

2 May

GIVE ALL THAT YOU CAN

Question: What is the proper attitude for an employee to have toward an employer?

Sri Gurudev: Gratefulness. He or she is employing you. He is giving you the opportunity to serve and is taking care of your welfare by giving you a salary. You need that employer. If you were not there the employer would still have a business, but you would not have a job. So the employee should always be grateful to the employer and honestly fulfill the duties he has been given.

Don't always think about how much the employer is giving you; think about how much you should give. Give all that you can. If you honestly do that, you will melt his heart. Even the hard-hearted employer will give you everything that you need, probably even more than you need. You will have won the employer, not just the salary.

3 May

I AM TAKING CARE OF ALL THESE PEOPLE

Question: Please speak on the relationship between the employer and employee.

Sri Gurudev: In a way, each depends on the other. If there's no employee, there's no employer. If there's no employer, there's no employee. The only difference is "er" and "ee." So the employer should know that if he or she doesn't take care of the employees, he cannot survive; he cannot grow. He should think, "Yes, it's an opportunity for me to serve the people. God has given me some wealth, some intelligence, and with these I am doing a job; through this business, I am taking care of all these people." He should feel, "I am serving them," not that he is helping them. God is the only one who can help us all; so each of us serves the other. And the employer should not take all the money and go to Las Vegas. He should convert that money by giving it back to the employees and taking care of their welfare so that they can keep working. It's a mutual give and take. Each one, employer and employee, should think of the welfare of the other.

4 May

GET INTO THEIR BOAT

Question: How do I know the difference between going with the flow and being out of control?

Sri Gurudev: That's where you should learn to apply moderation; be neither too tight nor too loose. If you can't figure it out by yourself, seek the aid of someone who can help you. Consult a more experienced person. Every situation you come across will be different.

When you say go with the flow, do you mean the flow of the world? If so, then that's not a good idea. Don't just go with the flow of the world. Go with the flow of the people who are going in the right direction. Join them. Get into their boat. The company you choose will help you in many, many ways.

Unfortunately, in the name of making a little money or feeding ourselves, we sometimes put ourselves in a terrible situation, or in the wrong atmosphere. We think that finding a little food and getting some money are the most important things. It's not so. Saving yourself, raising your standards, serving others, maintaining your peace—these are the most important things in life. For the sake of these things, you should learn to give up anything that's not necessary and to hold onto anything that is useful.

If you really want to go with the flow of God, surrender yourself completely to Him. That requires real courage. Surrendering is not easy. You have to positively say, "Whatever comes to me is God's will. I'm ready to face it, ready to accept it whatever it is—good or bad, wonderful or terrible."

5 May

MEASURE YOUR WORDS

I always recommend speaking with measured words—not going to the extremes of either complete silence or constant talking. Speak only when there is a need, and even then measure your words. Talking takes a lot of energy; and unnecessary speaking creates a lot of problems. You often make enemies by talking too much.

Occasionally observing silence for a time is a great practice. Silence is golden. Silence saves. I would recommend that practice to everyone.

6 May

FIRST YOU HAVE TO STABILIZE YOURSELF

Question: Can a spiritually-minded person have a harmonious life together with someone who is not spiritually-minded? The person I care about does not understand or accept my God-centeredness.

Sri Gurudev: You can still care about that person. Just remember that you have to stabilize yourself before you help someone else. Ideally, your companion should be somebody who has similar thinking; but if you are strong enough and won't be affected by his or her lifestyle, it's fine to stay with that person. Gradually you can help him. If you are going to be adversely affected by that person, you are not yet ready to be helpful; in that case, you should take care of yourself first. You can pray for that person, but don't let him disturb your peace.

7 May

BE WORRYLESS

Preparation for sleep is more important than sleeping itself. As soon as you walk into the house, don't just jump into bed and expect to get a good night's sleep. First release your soles from your shoes, have a nice shower, and put on some loose, comfortable clothing. As you loosen your body, loosen your mind also. Don't worry about tomorrow. Know that you have done today's job within your capacity. Talk to God: "God, by Your grace I have done something today, and I think I have finished my day. If You want me to do something tomorrow, I know You will wake me up. If You think I haven't done my job well and I'm just creating more problems, let my sleep be longer."

Know that if God wants you to get up, you will get up the next day. With that, resign yourself completely and just relax. That will happen only when you put your trust in something higher. God sent you here; He is working through you; He has done today's job. He may use you tomorrow. Be worryless like a baby. Don't put too much responsibility on your shoulders.

8 May

WHAT WOULD PEOPLE BE SAYING ABOUT YOU?

If you died this minute, what would people be saying about you? If the majority of people would feel sorry about your departure, if they would feel they had gotten a lot of help from you and that you hadn't hurt anyone, then certainly God is happy with you and the gates of Heaven are open to you.

To get God's Grace means to get the grace of your neighbors. God doesn't need your worship and service directly. Worship the Creation, and you have worshipped God. Serve the Creation, and you have served God.

Let us think of these points and see if we can do something to make our life a little better, a little more peaceful, a little more useful. If it is not useful, at least let it be harmless. The essence of all religions is this: just be good and do good. Then God will be happy with you, and you will find real peace and joy in your life.

9 May

YOUR ONLY RESPONSIBILITY

When we want to understand God's Will, God has a way of helping us subdue our ego. In a way, ego is always dependent on the spirit. We are never independent in that respect. But once we consciously submit ourselves completely to that spirit, then we are independent because God's will takes over. Then instead of saying, "I am doing it," the ego will say, "I am an instrument. I am being used by His Will." You recognize that He is doing everything. There is nothing for you to do. There is no responsibility for you. Your only responsibility is to surrender yourself into His hands and allow Him to do everything. That means allow the Consciousness to function through you.

10 May

"THE KING MIGHT PUNISH YOU IMMEDIATELY"

There is a proverb: "The king might punish you immediately if you get caught. If you escape, God will punish you in time."

You can never escape from Divine law. Don't ever forget that.

11 May

GOD IS HONORING YOU

Question: How can a devotee honor God?

Sri Gurudev: The Lord doesn't look for your honor. If you want to honor God, make Him happy by expressing His image, that part of God that is functioning in you. Put yourself into His hands. As the Bhagavad Gita proclaims, "Whatever you do, whatever you enjoy, whatever penance you perform, in essence everything that you think, speak or do, do it as an offering to God." Sri Krishna tells Arjuna, "Do it as an offering to me." God isn't asking for something of yours to be offered to Him. If it's yours, why should He ask for it? The truth is, nothing belongs to us. Even our thoughts and ideas. Everything happens due to His presence in this frame. Without God's energy, without God's Will, you cannot even think. The intelligence that you seem to possess is not yours; it's part of God's intelligence. The breath that you breathe is part of God's. The water that you drink belongs to God. The food that you eat belongs to God. Everything already belongs to God. So what is it that you are offering?

Then why should Krishna say, "Do it as an offering to me"? He is saying, "If you *feel* that they are yours, at least offer them to me." But it is even better to recognize that they never were yours. Ultimately you realize, "There's nothing for me to offer. On the other hand, *You* are the one who is doing everything through me. Even the offering is done by You to You." That way we really honor God. When you reach the highest level, you feel, "Everything already belongs to You. What is it that I am offering You? The only way to honor You is to *know* that You are honoring me by using me as Your instrument. At any time You can turn off the switch. I am thankful that You are still using me; You haven't discarded me as a blunt tool." Your vision takes a 180-degree turn. Instead of your honoring God, you realize that God is honoring you every minute.

12 May

THE SAME FOR ONE AND ALL

Enlightenment is the same for one and all. Is the sun in Australia different from the sun in America? There is the same sun, the same light, the same rain, the same air. Is there a man's sleep and a woman's sleep, a dog's sleep and a cat's sleep? No. Sleep is the same. Death is the same. Enlightenment also is the same. It doesn't differ at all from one person to the next. The only difference would be in how long it takes to come to that experience. But the experience is the same. At least we are all united in that.

13 May

THE QUICKEST WAY

Question: What is the surest, safest and quickest way to God-realization?

Sri Gurudev: The surest, safest and quickest way is to realize that God is working through you. The moment you realize that, you have realized already. Know that you are just an instrument in the hands of God. It's a fact. I wouldn't even say that you *give* yourself into the hands of God. Who are you to give? You are already His instrument. Just know that.

14 May

CONSTANTLY WINNING IS BORING

Life is a sport. Everything that you do is a game. Play each game well. Don't worry about competing; just play your best. And don't always look to win. Constantly winning is boring. Treat everything as equal: victory and failure, profit and loss. Enjoy them both. If you win a thousand dollars, say, "Great! I won a thousand dollars." If you lose a thousand dollars, say, "Look at that! I lost a thousand dollars. Great!" That way, even if you lose a thousand dollars, you won't lose your mind along with it. So play well, but remember that it's all a game.

15 May

CLEAN MONEY

Don't work thinking only of your salary. If God is satisfied with your work, He will give you plenty. You will get your salary, and more, from many other sources. Think of your job as an opportunity to serve, not just an opportunity to make money. If you work with that serviceful attitude, then whatever you make will be clean money, well-earned money that will certainly bring health and happiness to you. It's not how *much* money we make, but *how* we make it that's important.

God knows how to adjust things. Sometimes we get into some unexpected trouble. You lose something, break something, or fall sick and give hundreds of dollars to the doctors. Why? Because the money that you earned was not clean, so it has to be taken away by someone. If we can earn clean money we won't have these problems.

Clean money comes from honest work. What you give should be at least a little more than what you get. That is what you call karma yoga. It will make the money that comes to you into clean money.

16 May

THE WORLD WILL ALWAYS BE LIKE THIS

Don't expect the whole world to be enlightened one day. It would be like walking into a Detroit automobile factory and seeing only finished cars. If the factory were full of finished cars, it would no longer be a factory; it would become a showroom. Likewise, you wouldn't go to a university and say, "When will the only people here be degree holders?"

The universe itself is a university. People come as students; they study and learn. A few people get their diplomas and walk out. The world will always be like this. Don't think that one day the whole world will be enlightened. It is not possible. There will always be people who are still learning. When you understand the world, and realize your own true nature, you get the diploma. When others see you enjoying the peace and joy of having acquired that diploma, they will be inspired by you and will also work hard to get one. That is the world.

17 May

I BELIEVE IN MEDICINE ALSO

Question: Is it interfering with one's karma to take medicine?

Sri Gurudev: I believe in prayer, but I believe in medicine also. Medicine is also a gift from God. Prayer, medicine, and certain dietetic disciplines all could be used at the same time. Even food could be considered a medicine for the pain of hunger. If you believe in prayer, the hunger should just go away. If you eat, then why can't you take medicine also? Prayer is one form of healing. We can use all the possible ways.

The important thing is, don't let others do everything for your sake. You should also do something. When people send their prayer requests here, we ask them also to pray at the same time. It's not, "You do whatever you want, I'll pray for you and you will get well." That's not right. That *is* interfering with karma. The people who are affected should also go through certain disciplines in life. The pain comes to make you believe in a higher spirit, a higher power.

There is nothing wrong with looking for some remedy for a problem. If your karma is that strong, even with all the remedies, it won't get cured. Then you know, yes, your karma is stronger than that. Accept it. But when somebody comes and offers, "Shall I help you?", then your karma is bringing somebody to help you. Accept it.

18 May

HAVE CONVICTION

What you think you become. That is why it is so important to have positive thoughts. But if you merely repeat something without any feeling behind it, it's just mechanical. You have to have some conviction: "I *am* becoming joyful. I *am* becoming brave. Day by day I am becoming better and better." By the same token, if you say, "Oh, I don't think I can do it. I am growing weaker. I'm not any good," then you are dwelling on negative thoughts. So think about what kind of food you are feeding your thoughts. Give them good, nourishing food. Don't give them poison. Then they will become powerful instruments for good in the world.

19 May

TAKE CARE OF THE LITTLE, LITTLE THINGS

Often people think that spirituality only means big things, that to be a spiritual aspirant you must accomplish great feats. You should chant beautifully; you should stand on your head for half an hour; you should sit for meditation three times a day. These things are wonderful, but they are not useful if you don't take care of the little, little things. Spirituality should permeate every action of your day. By simply going into your room and seeing its condition, people can tell how much rubbish there is inside your mind.

20 May

IT'S A POWERFUL SEED

In this age, the simplest and best practice is mantra repetition. It is very simple, but at the same time very powerful—more powerful than any other practice. Your body may not even be fit to practice all the hatha yoga postures or to do rigorous penance. You may not have a lot of money to go on pilgrimages. You may not have a big altar or go to church every Sunday, but you can always repeat a mantram. Wherever you are, whatever you do, whether you are rich or poor, it doesn't matter. Repeating the mantram is like cultivating a seed. It's a powerful seed that, once planted, will slowly take root and grow in you. In the beginning you have to nurture it carefully and regularly. Then it will grow into a beautiful, big, divine tree and bring forth much fruit. Certainly the whole world will enjoy that fruit.

21 May

THE BEST THING WE CAN DO

Don't ever, ever put yourself down. You are here for a purpose, and you are great in your place. You may not know what that purpose is; but no matter what you look like, what handicaps you might have, what size or what color you are, the fact that you are here is enough. God has something for you to do. Let us always live in that knowledge. Let us become humble instruments in the hands of that great Lord. That's the best thing we can do. He will take care of all the rest.

WHAT AM I DOING IT FOR?

Just be happy, have fun, enjoy life and don't get caught. When I say, "don't get caught," I am not talking about someone else catching you. I am talking about your own mind. Choose the kind of fun that won't bind you. If a certain kind of fun will bring you unhappiness later on, then it's not fun at all. Our goal is *unending* joy.

Sometimes people think that to be a spiritual seeker or a good, religious person means being always very serious. They think that such a person can't have fun, can't laugh. That is no kind of life. Life means being always joyful, always happy, jubilant. Every minute should be a celebration. Every minute should be a festivity. That is possible only if you keep your mind in good shape and don't allow it to get into mischief.

Be conscious of all your actions. Before you do anything, question yourself: "What am I doing it for? To be happy, to have fun. Okay, will it be fun always or will it only be fun for a little while and then start creating problems? Will anyone be hurt by it? How long can I be happy? Will there be an end? What is the price I have to pay?" After all this analysis, if your answer is, "Yes. I will always be happy. It will never bind or bother me," then go ahead. Remember, our intention is to enjoy life, to be happy always—nothing less than that.

23 May

YOU ARE SPIRIT

Your true personality is happiness; it is peace and love. The minute you forget that, you start to look for these things to come from outside. Unfortunately that has happened even from the very beginning. When God made Adam, He told him, "Adam, I have created you in My own image. That means you are Me; I am you. There is no difference at all. Have you ever seen Me unhappy? No. In the same way, you are never unhappy. You are happiness personified. Have you ever seen Me hungry, thirsty? No. In the same way, you are never hungry or thirsty because you are spirit. Hunger and thirst are physical phenomena; the body has that experience. *You* are not the body. You are not even the mind. You are the spirit. You *are* happiness, and you can always retain your happiness if you don't forget that."

24 May

TAKE IT AS A CHALLENGE

Question: What should a person do if her family members are against her spiritual pursuits?

Sri Gurudev: Take it as a challenge, and know that God is on your side. You don't need to hate them. Instead, you should take it as a good omen. God has put an examiner right next to you to test how strong you are in your convictions. He has really seen your thirst in spiritual life, and He wants to make sure that you are really serious about it.

Don't you have to pass a big test before you are graduated? It's true. So don't think of those people as negative. An examiner is not a negative person. Your family has so much love for you; if they seem to be negative to you, don't be negative to them in return. Just because you are together, it doesn't mean that you have the same growth in understanding life. Each soul grows in its own way. The others may still be young in their growth; all you can do is be patient and prove the benefit of your practice by your own example.

Eventually the others will ask, "Honey, how come you are so peaceful and so happy, even when I am nasty toward you?" Then you can say, "Well, just a little bit of spiritual practice helps me." That's enough. Leave it there. Don't push. Allow them to grow; one day they might even excel you. Very often it happens that way.

So prove by your own example that you are becoming a beautiful person. Don't argue; instead, let them see that you are being helped by what you are doing. They will be watching you. When your own life shows the wonderful benefits of your practice, they will say, "Honey, I misunderstood. I'm sorry. I see how healthy and happy this has made you." Until that time, be patient. As a spiritual person, you should see that there is harmony present in the family in all situations.

25 May

WHAT YOU GAIN, YOU SHOULD NOT LOSE

Never give up. Know that your spiritual goal is something great. You have fallen down from the summit, and you are on your way back up. It is greater even than climbing Mount Everest. As soon as the climbers get to the peak of Everest, they have to go down again. They never rest. But with the spiritual climb, once you get there you rest there forever.

This is the highest peak. Just go on, steadily climbing. If you get tired, if you see some dense clouds coming, if there is no visibility, set up camp. But don't go back to the base. Every time you need to stop, set up camp there. When the mountain climbers cannot continue, do they go back to the bottom and start over again the next day? No. What you gain, you should not lose. Whenever necessary, stop, build yourself up, regain your strength; and when the storm has cleared, continue to go forward.

The mind also has storms. Sometimes the storm is so violent that nothing seems to help; not even reading scriptures or repeating your mantram. It doesn't matter; just don't give up. Stay in the camp and wait for the storm to pass. Make a resolution, "I will march forward a step at a time, no matter how slowly. I am never going to turn back. Even if I am not going to achieve anything in this life, it doesn't matter. I'll continue in the next life and the one after that, and the one after *that*. Never, never will I turn back." That kind of courage is necessary. It's a big task. The hardest thing in the world is to train one's own mind.

26 May

ONE DAY THAT GREATNESS WILL LEAP FORWARD IN YOU

Training the mind is worth doing at any cost. It's extremely difficult. That's why we don't see very many saints. If it were that easy, there would be thousands. How many saints have there been like that? You can easily count them.

Don't be discouraged; don't think that you shouldn't try for it. How do you know that you are not going to be a Buddha? How do you know that there is no Christhood or no Buddhahood in you? One day, all of a sudden, that greatness will leap forward in you. Don't give up. Never give up hope.

27 May

HE IS ALWAYS HELPING YOU

Through both pleasure and pain, God is trying to help you grow in the right direction. Keep in mind that He is always behind everything; He is always helping you. If you put your complete trust in God, your mind will not even come up with desires that might hurt you unnecessarily.

28 May

DON'T EXPECT SOMEONE ELSE TO DO ALL THE WORK

Question: If we have faith in God, do we need medicine when we are sick?

Sri Gurudev: Medicine is also a gift from God. Prayer, medicine, and certain dietetic discipline could all be used at the same time. Even food is a kind of medicine for the pain of hunger. Do you say that if you believe in prayer, then you should not feel hunger? No. If you eat to relieve hunger, you can also take advantage of medical science when necessary. We can use all the things God has given us, as long as we use them properly.

Whatever method of healing you use, don't expect someone else to do all the work for you. A doctor shouldn't just give a pill and say, "Go ahead—smoke all you want, continue to overeat, drink all the alcohol you want and don't exercise. This pill will make you better." No. If necessary, the patient can have some medicine, but he or she should make whatever changes are needed to have good health. When people send prayer requests to us, we ask them to pray also. It isn't: "You go ahead and do whatever you want. I'll pray for you and you'll get well." That's not right. That's interfering with someone's karma. The people who are affected should practice certain disciplines.

There is nothing wrong in looking for some remedy for a problem. If your karma is really strong, even with all the remedies, the ailment won't get cured. If that happens, you should know it's because of some karma and accept it. If somebody comes to help you, then your karma is bringing somebody to help. You should accept that too.

IT'S A BIG DEMAND

When you are on a pilgrimage, you depend totally on God. You don't depend on your credit cards, your hotel bookings, your taxis. Nothing. You just give yourself into the hands of God. "God, I'm coming to You completely empty-handed. You do anything You want with me." There is a great benefit in that. Only then do you realize that He is with you every minute. You feel God as you would feel your own breath, your own heartbeat. Even one little distraction is enough to keep you from experiencing that presence.

Saint Ramakrishna gave a very beautiful, very simple example of this. When you want to thread a needle, you have to insert all of the fibers at the same time. If even one tiny fiber sticks out, the thread won't go in. All of the fibers must be well twisted and concentrated; then it is easy to thread the needle.

So if even one little fiber gets distracted, separated from your concentration, that will prevent you from entering into God. It's very difficult to achieve this kind of concentration. That's why you don't see many great sages and saints around. How many are ready to give up all these little distractions for God?

30 May

AT LEAST YOU SHOULD KNOW WHY YOU ARE NOT SEEING GOD

Once a young man went to Sri Ramakrishna and said, "Sir, I want to see God right away."

Sri Ramakrishna said, "Before you see God we will go to the Ganges so you can take a bath." He took the young man to the Ganges and said, "All right, dip." But when he dipped into the water, Sri Ramakrishna held him under. Immediately the devotee started fighting for his breath. When the saint realized that he would not be able to stay under the water any longer, he let him up.

As the young man stood gasping on the riverbank, Sri Ramakrishna asked him, "What were you thinking while you were in the water? Were you thinking of your money, your wife, your son, your name, your fame, your profession?"

"All I was thinking about was a little air!"

"Aha. When you can think of God like that, you'll see Him right away."

Now you know what kind of one-pointed yearning for God is required. I don't expect everyone to get to that point right away, but at least you should know why you are not seeing God. You can't blame anyone else for it. Although sometimes people try to. They blame the technique or the teacher or the mantram. You really don't even need any technique, any mantram, anything, if you have that kind of one-pointed mind.

UNITY IN DIVERSITY

In essence we are one, but in nonsense we are many. We need essence and nonsense. Life is for fun; otherwise God could have just created everyone alike with the same thoughts. Everything is God's Will. Nothing happens without His Will. He allows this chaos. Why? He must have thought, "Only by this chaotic situation will they really thirst for peace. Then, if I give them peace, they will really relish it."

That is why we are looking for peace. We have had enough of fights and problems. If you realize this, you can begin right in your own home. Love your family, your pets, your plants. Do not treat them as something different from yourself. They all have the same essence, the same spirit. If we want to show the unity in diversity, that is where we can begin. At home, with our pots and pans. You may be angry with your husband or wife, but do not put the pot down with a bang. Be gentle. See the same spirit in everything. That is unity in diversity. There is nothing without life in this world. Be gentle, be nice, be loving. See your own Self in all and treat everything properly. That is how to show the unity in diversity visibly and powerfully. A real spiritual experience means to see the unity in diversity.

June

1 June

PEACE IS GOD

In the Bhagavad Gita, Sri Krishna says, "Think of Me always." When He says, "Think of Me," it should be taken as, "Think of God," because it is God who speaks in the name of Krishna. So "Think of God;" but how can you think of God without knowing what God is? We don't know what God is. All that we know *about* God is not really God. We only think in terms of what we have heard or read or assumed. In yogic understanding, what is God? Peace. Peace is God. So think of peace always. That means, remember that there is always peace in you. Think of your positive nature. Always affirm, "I am peaceful, I am joyful," and act accordingly. If you constantly think in that way, then you won't be running after things to be happy. That is the thought that we should constantly keep in mind. All other thoughts are the outcome of forgetting this truth.

2 June

YOU ARE WHAT YOU THINK

You are what you think. Remember that. If your thoughts are impure, then your body is sick, your mind is sick, your life is sick. You may have all kinds of medicine around your house, hundreds of doctors to take care of you; but they cannot help you if you are poisoning your system with wrong thoughts. As you think, so you become. Thoughts are very important.

3 June

WHAT IS A VOW?

What is a vow? Your own commitment. You decide to do a certain thing, to follow certain principles, and that becomes your vow. You make a vow. A marriage vow is a commitment. A monastic vow is a commitment. Even friendship is a commitment. Life itself is a commitment.

If you make a vow and honestly try, and find you cannot live up to it, you need not feel guilty about it. Because if you feel guilty then you lose your courage, your strength of mind. But if you make a promise to somebody and if you fail in your promise and by that you affect someone else's life, then certainly you will feel guilty and the karma will affect you.

Without commitment in life we can never grow. Commitment is a way of training the mind and making it obey you. You become the master of your mind. Who wants to break the commitment? Your mind. The mind pops up, "Oh, I don't want to do it," and you give up. Then wherever you go, whatever you do, the mind will have that same tendency. Think before you leap. Once you leap, that's it. Stick to it, whatever it is. Your dynamic will should be applied. "Yes, I decided to do it. I am going to do it. I will never back out." The dynamic decision itself will help you achieve success in that.

4 June

ONE MEANS NO FEAR

A fearless person is the one who is afraid of God. What is meant by "fear of God?" Fear of God's law, or the Cosmic Law. That means you know the Cosmic Law, what action will bring what result, and you are afraid of doing a wrong action. Fear is created for that purpose. If you keep on doing the right thing, you come to see that you don't need to be afraid of anything. You become fearless. So begin with fear and ultimately become fearless.

The fear is necessary. When you go near a flame you know that it will burn, and you are careful. That is what you call fear. Knowing and staying away from the wrong is what you call fear. The real fearless state is when you see everyone as your own Self. When you see yourself in others, you are not afraid of them. In realizing that oneness, you rise above the fear totally. As long as there's duality, you are afraid. You are afraid of your own body sometimes, your own mind sometimes, because you see them as different than you. Two means fear. One means no fear. That spiritual oneness is to be recognized. Until then, we are afraid.

5 June

PRAYERFUL THOUGHTS ALWAYS BRING BENEFIT TO PEOPLE

Question: How should we pray? There seems to be a contradiction between totally trusting in God's Will and praying for someone or something.

Sri Gurudev: It is the same thing. There is no contradiction at all. But you should understand the purpose of your prayer. You don't go and ask God, "Give me that." If you feel you must ask for something, then say, "Please give me understanding. Give me the constant remembrance that You are handling everything, that You will give me everything I deserve, and You will never give anything to me if I don't deserve it." If God is going to do something only after you request it, what kind of God is that? "Oh, because ten people are praying for you, because I got ten thousand signatures, I am giving you this." No. But when ten thousand people feel sorry for a person and pray, all that wishful thinking goes to help him or her.

Good thoughts and feelings always reach the ones who are really starving for them. Those who really deserve that good thinking will receive it. We simply spread the seeds. When people know that so many others are praying for them, that gives them strength. There is a benefit right away, "Oh, so many people are praying for me. I should really get well. All their good thinking is on my side." Prayerful thoughts always bring benefit to people.

6 June

I'M NOT AFRAID, I'M NOT AFRAID, I'M NOT AFRAID

Question: Are great catastrophes, possibly even a nuclear war, in store for the world; and if so, what will happen to each of our individual evolving souls?

Sri Gurudev: First of all, "Are there catastrophes in store?" The answer is "Maybe." Oh, you wanted a year and date. Okay, "Maybe tomorrow." Remember—what God created can be destroyed. Don't ever forget that. What was put together will get separated one day. But don't *you* cut it. If at any time it has to be cut, let the One who put it together do the cutting. And don't worry about catastrophes. If something has to happen, let it happen. It's all up to Him.

"I'm not afraid, I'm not afraid, I'm not afraid! Even if the whole galaxy breaks into pieces and falls onto my head, I'm not afraid!" That was the song sung by a great saintly poet, Bharati. Don't worry about tomorrow. Today there's no catastrophe. Why worry about it? Enjoy the golden present.

7 June

IF YOU WANT TO COMMUNICATE WITH GOD

The very first created sound is OM. In a way, the unmanifested God first manifests as OM. So if you want to communicate with God, who is vibrating in this OM sound, you should be able to receive that vibration by tuning your heart radio to the same frequency. The radio should be tuned to the same frequency as the transmitting station. God is transmitting His energy, His beauty, His love, His grace, everything at this OM frequency. If you want to receive it, where should you tune your radio? To the same OM. That is why mantra meditation is a very important practice. All other practices are secondary when compared with mantra repetition. Mantra repetition is a direct way to tune yourself to that cosmic vibration. Even if you don't do any of the other practices you should not miss mantra repetition. That alone will help you a lot. Every day, at least three times—morning, noon and evening—if not more, you should produce that sound by repeating your mantram. Then you are tuning your radio constantly to stay on a certain wavelength.

8 June

WHAT IS PURITY OF HEART?

What is purity of heart? A heart full of tranquility, full of peace. Having a steady mind, a balanced mind, is what you call purity of heart. Being well-balanced between the dualities: the ups and downs, the pleasure and pain, the profit and loss. If the mind is free from turbulence, then the seer can see its own nature. If your heart is pure and steady, you can see God reflected in that steady heart.

YOU DON'T HAVE TO BE ALLERGIC TO ANYTHING

If you keep the body healthy, the body can adjust to any weather. You won't have to complain about the outside atmosphere. Many people complain about allergies. They are always saying, "I am allergic to this, allergic to that." Allergy is not something coming from outside; allergy comes from lack of health. If your body is strong enough, you don't have to be allergic to anything.

Think of all the people who live in a tropical climate where there is heat and humidity. Fortunately the body is able to accept any condition, to withstand and adapt, because it's made that way. How many people poison their systems, and their bodies accept it? The body even accepts smoking and drinking.

Keep the body in good shape. That means giving it the proper exercise and eating the right food in the right quantity. Above all, have the proper thoughts.

If you constantly complain of disease, you will have disease. As you think so you become. If you think, "I am weak, I am weak, I am weak," you are certainly going to be weak. Never allow the mind to worry about anything.

THAT'S WHY HE CAN STOP YOUR ELEPHANT

Once upon a time there lived a king who had a nice elephant. The attendant of the elephant used to take it to the river every day for a bath. One day as the attendant was bringing the elephant back to the palace, a little boy came walking up to the elephant. He took its trunk in his hands, saying, "Stop! Look at the way you are walking!" The elephant stopped. "Walk gently, carefully," he told the elephant. He let go of the trunk, and the elephant started walking again. The next day as the elephant passed the same spot, the boy came running and stopped the elephant to reprimand it again. This happened several days in a row.

The attendant couldn't believe what was happening. He told the king, who sent his minister to check on the boy. In a few days, the minister came to report to the king. "Sir, I observed the boy. He lives with his grandmother. He's just a playful little boy. He seems ordinary, but he has absolutely no fear. That's why he can stop your elephant."

"I can't believe it," said the king. "What do you mean?"

"Sir, a mind without fear and worry can do anything."

The king wanted the minister to prove his point. The only way to do so was to make the boy worry about something. The minister approached the boy's grandmother. After hearing from her that the boy was allowed to do anything he wanted, the minister asked, "Has he ever asked for anything and been refused?"

"No. I have given him everything that he wanted. He is just a happy-go-lucky boy."

"Is he afraid of anything?

"Nothing at all."

The minister had to prove his theory to the king, so he said, "All right. When he comes home today give him the usual food, but add less than the usual amount of salt. If the boy asks about it, tell him that you don't have enough money to buy salt, so you had to be sparing with what you have left."

The grandmother said, "If the king wants me to do that, I shall do it."

That evening when the boy came home, she served his supper right away. After a few bites, the boy said, "Grandma, what is this? It's not tasty today." The grandmother repeated what the minister had told her, and the boy said, "Okay, Grandmother, I will get you some salt." He ran to the shop and asked the shopkeeper to give him a little salt. The shopkeeper explained that he couldn't give him salt without receiving money in exchange.

"Where can I get some money?" the boy asked.

"You have to go and work for it."

"I don't know how to work."

"Then you can't get any salt."

The boy was a little depressed. He went home. "Grandma, I don't know what to do. He wants me to go and work and get money so I can get some salt. I don't know how to work."

"All right, sweetheart," said the grandmother, "it doesn't matter. Go to sleep. We'll talk about it tomorrow."

The boy went to bed, but he couldn't sleep all night. In the morning, the elephant came as usual, and as usual, the boy went to stop the elephant, but he couldn't do it. The elephant pushed him aside and walked off. All the young fellow had in mind was, "I couldn't get a little salt for my food." That one small worry had taken away all his strength.

11 June

HUNDREDS OF WORRIES

How many wants do you have? How many things do you worry about? "I don't have this." "I didn't get that." "I don't have a nice enough office." "I didn't get the car I wanted." "I don't have an air conditioner." "I didn't get what I wanted to eat." There are all kinds of unnecessary worries. Hundreds and hundreds and hundreds of worries. How can you lift even a small blade of grass with that kind of attitude?

The mind is the main source of health and happiness. The same mind can completely rob you of all your health and happiness if you don't train it properly. Heat, humidity, cold, hunger—all these conditions are nothing if your mind is calm and balanced.

12 June

IT'S GOD'S CHILD GIVEN IN YOUR CARE

A mother's first and foremost duty is her child. Everything else comes afterward. A beautiful soul has been given into your hands. You should sacrifice anything and everything for the sake of that child. Don't neglect your child to do other duties. All other duties are nothing compared to this. All other duties should be conducive to fulfilling this duty; it's not at the cost of this duty that you do other things. The world can wait. The child needs you. The world may not need you. Take care of the child. And if you know your responsibility and think, "Yes, God has given me this opportunity, I have to do it and I'm going to do it," you will get strength. God gave the child in your care, and He will give you enough strength to fulfill that duty also. He is not a fool that would put a child in weak hands. You may not know your own strength. God will never give a baby to a mother or father who cannot take care of it. So realize that you have the strength. Believe in that and go ahead, take care of that beautiful angel. Raise that child up into a beautiful, spiritual child of God.

SHOUT FOR HELP

If you need God's help, just be spontaneous. If you feel like crying to Him, cry. Shout for help. All the great saints, all their prayers, were literally shouting to God for help. "God, have mercy on me!"

If you say that even once with your entire heart, you're sure to get His help immediately. God knows whether you are calling for His help sincerely or not. When you look for God, you should know nothing else is going to help you. Sincere prayer comes only when you are tired of everything, when you know fully well that nothing else but God will save you. As long as you depend on yourself a little, God waits.

14 June

SLOWLY THE GRIP LOOSENS

In India, during the summer, people drink a lot of coconut water. They just make a small opening in the coconut and drink the liquid that's inside. There is also a nice, tasty jelly inside, the tender kernel before it hardens; but it takes a big machete to open the shell. Sometimes people don't have a big machete so they just drink the water and throw the rest of the coconut away.

When the monkeys see a discarded coconut, they know that there is something nice inside. One of them will come, slowly put a hand inside, and grab that tender kernel. But when the monkey tries to pull its hand back out, the hand gets caught. You see? The hand is now a fist clutching the prize and it's bigger than when it went in. The monkey screams and runs around, but still it holds onto the kernel. Sometimes the monkey's wrist will even get cut and bleed. Still, it won't let go because it's eager to eat that treat. It continues to hold the kernel tight, and continues to run around screaming, screaming, screaming.

At last the monkey gets really tired and stops running; but it still holds on. Finally when it is so exhausted that it loses its capacity to do anything, slowly the grip loosens and the hand slips out.

Many of us are like those monkeys. We hold some attachment tightly and say, "I don't want it! I don't want it! I'm tired. I want to get out of this!" When you are really tired, you will let go.

15 June

DAY TURNS INTO NIGHT, NIGHT TURNS INTO DAY

Never be afraid of anything. A person with fear dies every minute. Remember that. Know that change is a part of nature. Things will always come and go, join and separate, make again and break again. Daily you see that. The sun rises and sets. Day turns into night, night turns into day. Remember, even when there have been catastrophes, this world has still gone on. And it still continues.

How big is your world? Do you think it's a *big* world? If you compare your world to the entire cosmos, your world is not even equal to one hundredth of a mustard seed, remember that. By the time I answer your question, do you know how many worlds like this will be reduced to pieces somewhere in the galaxy? Every minute stars fall, planets are destroyed and then rebuilt again. I remember someone once asked a scientist, "How big is our world? How many galaxies are there in the whole cosmos?" Do you know what he said? There was a big, beautiful, shaggy dog with long hair sitting nearby and the scientist said,"If you shave all of this dog's hair as close to the skin as possible, and then chop the hairs into tiny, tiny pieces, and count those pieces you will have counted one hundredth of the total galaxies in the cosmos." Can you perceive that number? The mind cannot even begin to grasp it.

So don't worry about these changes. Today you are happy and comfortable, and if you can do something to make someone else also happy and comfortable, do it. If you cannot do it, at least don't make others miserable. If you can't make others happy, at least don't make them unhappy by thinking about catastrophes, and this and that. Even if everything breaks up, *you* will remain. What is that "you?" The unbreakable one, the soul, your consciousness, which you call the Self. That always remains because consciousness never changes. The consciousness is always there, but it expresses itself in various ways using various forms, being called by various names. So as the Self, you are immortal. Don't be afraid of anything. *You* are eternal.

16 June

IT ALL DEPENDS UPON WHETHER YOU BELIEVE IT

Question: How do we know if flipping a coin to make a decision will reflect God's Will?

Sri Gurudev: You are only flipping the coin. You do not make it fall this way or that. The coin will fall to the heads side or tails side by itself. Just think that the falling is in God's hands. Tossing is your business. Dropping it to the right side is His business. The whole of life is a game. When you want to take sides in a game, what do you do? You flip a coin to decide who's on which team. The tennis players rotate the racquet. Even in this so-called modern, scientific space age, we still flip coins. What does it mean? It means that there is an unseen force; things don't just happen in an uncontrolled way. Somebody is controlling it. So it depends upon whether you believe that every movement is controlled by a higher will or not. If you believe it, yes, it's God's Will. If you don't believe it, it is yours.

17 June

THE SIMPLEST TEACHING

Being a good disciple or a spiritual person, or experiencing the Truth, doesn't depend on your learning or your capability of performing asanas or your skill in chanting. Those things are all good no doubt, but they are not the end-all. If you have it, fine. But the real mark of spiritual life is the thirst for knowledge. You cry for God.

The Upanishads say, "Not by doing a lot of things, not by acquiring book knowledge, not even by charity, not by progeny, not by any of these things can we experience that great Truth, the immortal principle, but by total, total renunciation, total dedication." A mind completely free from any sort of "I, me, mine," is the one and only qualification. "*Tyagat shanthir anantaram.*" That means that God in the form of *shanthi*—peace—will reside in you always. And you will be able to experience that only when you have *tyaga*—dedication—in your life. Renounce the selfishness. This is the teaching. All the other things are there just to keep the student busy.

If you come one day and I say, "This is all: Renounce your selfishness and you will realize the Self," then you will say, "What is this? I went there and I wanted to learn something. He simply told me this and sent me out. He didn't teach me scriptures, hatha yoga. I never learned to stand on my head." All these things are simply to keep you engaged in something so that you don't get into trouble. But none of these things will help you in experiencing the highest truth if there is no renunciation of selfishness.

18 June

IT IS BETTER TO LEARN SOON

Even if you achieve the whole world by your selfishness, you are not going to be happy. You cannot be. Selfishness can never make you happy. Sometimes you may get what you want, but your own selfishness will spoil it. In a way, that is what we learn from all these disappointments in life. Every time you approach a thing or a person or an action with a selfish motive, it literally hits you on the head. Unfortunately many people don't learn from a single hit or even a hundred hits. On the other hand, sensible people will learn the lesson just by seeing others getting hit.

Don't ever think that you will escape. You are going to learn the lesson. Until you learn the lesson this will happen again and again and again. Mother Nature is there with a big stick to whack you, "Come on, learn this, learn this." Finally you will say, "Ohh, I am learning, I am learning."

You should remember it is Mother Nature's hand behind all these disappointments. So it is better to learn soon—the sooner, the better—so that you can enjoy the rest of your life with all joy and peace.

19 June

THE BEST FORM OF DEVOTION

The best way to communicate with the higher Self, or God, is to say: "I am thinking of You. I am repeating Your holy name. I am trying to develop that holy vibration in me. That's all I know. And I know that You know the rest. I am not asking for anything. I don't even know what to ask for. I might even ask for the wrong thing, for something that may not help me. Or I might ask for too little and You'll say, 'Well, that's all that you asked for.' Even though You may want to give me more, if I ask for a little You will give me only that. So I leave it up to You; You know what is best. If You think that I am doing something right or doing it wrong, You will let me know. You are really the Father of fathers, and 'Father knows best!' I am cleaning my house and preparing for Your arrival to take residence. Please come and give whatever You want, whenever You want, however you want. I leave all that to You."

That is the best form of communication. We shouldn't be demanding, expecting, even imagining. Simply say, "I am doing my job, I know You will do Your job." The best form of devotion is that.

20 June

WHO IS HUGGING HER NOW?

Once a pretty young girl was stung by a scorpion. It happened on a mountain top, at evening time. To go to the clinic down below, you had to descend a thousand steps. There were mostly monks and spiritual aspirants around, and everyone was trying to figure out what to do. The girl was lying on the ground crying, and her mother also was crying. A renunciate is not supposed to touch a girl, so the monks were planning to get a stretcher or something on which to move her. As they were planning, I said, "This is all foolishness." I grabbed her, put her on my shoulder and ran down the hill to the clinic. The doctor immediately gave her an injection, after which she calmed down and fell asleep. But all the people around started gossiping, "Look at that swami. How could he carry a girl like that? Look at the way he hugged her." For four or five days this was bubbling, and it slowly reached my Gurudev, Swami Sivanandaji. During his next talk he looked at the *sannyasis* and said, "Ahh. Who is hugging the girl now? You or him? True, he carried her down the hill, but he put her down at the clinic. All of you are still carrying her."

HE GIVES YOU WHAT YOU WANT

I read a beautiful piece of wisdom recently: "When God wants to punish you, He will give you everything that you ask for." He gives you what *you* want, even though it may not be good for you. Unfortunately, we still don't know what to want. We want many, many things; we want all the things that bring us problems. So we are the cause of our problems. When someone has a problem you say, "Ahh, he asked for it." We don't even know what to ask for. So the best prayer would be, "God, I don't know what to ask for. I may even ask for the wrong thing, I'm still a child. As a good father, good mother, You know what is beneficial for me. You give me what I need. Please don't give me what I want. I will accept whatever You give me. And I will accept what You take away from me. You are the giver, You are the taker." If you allow God to take things from you whenever He wants, you will never make a mistake in your life.

What is God's duty? To give the proper result for your action. That is nature's law. Then why does God allow people who do good things to suffer and people who do bad things to get what they want? Those people are good now, but they were not good before. And the others once did something to deserve what they are getting now, even though it might have been long before. That is an important point that we miss in the West. We are slowly beginning to understand that, "Yes, we lived before and we will be still living after." There is life before birth, and life after death. The soul is immortal. It simply goes through different bodies to gain more experiences. You carry all your past actions and their results with you.

YOUR GOOD ACTIONS WILL BRING GOOD RESULTS LATER ON

What we earned in the previous life we bring to this life. And in this life we are earning more. If we have done a lot of bad actions before, and suffered the results, we learned, "Yes, I shouldn't be doing anything bad." Now you are a good person, but that doesn't mean that all of the bad things you did before are going to be forgotten. No. You have to answer for them. You are good now, you were bad before. So your sufferings are the result of your past bad actions. Your good actions will bring good results later on. But if you don't believe in that you say, "Oh, why is a good man suffering like this? Look at that bad man, he is enjoying life." He was good before, so he enjoys all that now. If he doesn't have time to face the results of his present actions in this very life itself, he will certainly face them in the next life. That is the theory of karma. No one can escape from that.

So God is not responsible for the karma. God is only responsible for seeing that what you sow, you reap. That's all. If you put your finger in the fire, it will burn you. The fire is not responsible for that. The function of fire is to burn. You can use the fire for a good purpose or for a bad purpose. It's up to you. So let us not blame God for everything. God is a neutral energy, like electricity. Plug in a lamp, you get light. Plug in your finger, you get a shock. You cannot label electricity as good or bad. You can use it for any purpose.

23 June

SERVE ONE AND ALL

Question: What is the best way to serve God while living in the world?

Sri Gurudev: Serve one and all. Then you will have served God. Don't even lose a single opportunity to serve others. Serve, serve, serve, and you will find that you also are served.

24 June

THIS WILL SAVE YOU FROM A LOT OF PROBLEMS

When you cannot avoid certain things, the easiest way to bring peace into your heart is to immediately accept them. "*Kita dayin, vetana mara*" is a beautiful Tamil saying that means, "If you cannot get it, immediately forget it." Remembering this will save you from a lot of problems. If you deserve something, let it come to you. Accept whatever is given to you by God, and accept whatever is taken away from you by God.

25 June

WHAT IS HEAVEN?

Heaven is a place where love and nothing but love flows. Real, cosmic, universal love. People love each other as they love themselves. They love the animals, the plants, all the things around them. They even love their trash cans. That's what heaven is. Everyone living as one big family with no "mine" and "yours," only "ours." It's God's home and everyone feels that they are children of that home. Everything is common. Everybody takes care of every thing.

It's a collective life. Even if one individual is unhappy, everybody takes care of that person and sees that he or she becomes happy again. Our property is common, our money is common, our kitchen is common, our school is common. In a way, everything belongs to everybody. That's how people live in heaven.

If we could live that way, certainly we would have a heaven here. And that is exactly what yogic life means. Living a collective life. Rising above selfishness. Sharing the joy of everyone, and the pain of everyone. Of course such a thing may not happen overnight. It might take a lot of effort because we have been brought up with this "I, me, mine, that's mine, that's yours," consciousness. We have to slowly undo all that now.

We have our independence, our individuality; but our independence should not interfere with the independence of others. Different individuals live together like the flowers in a bouquet. They may appear to be different, but they have a common purpose: serving each other and collectively serving humanity. That is our aim. Whatever we do should be done in this light.

26 June

WE CAN ALWAYS BE IN BLISS

Whatever you are, be contented. It sounds good but it's not so easy. If you have a contented mind, everything will just happen by itself. You won't have to *do* anything. Somebody is doing everything through you. You have nothing to worry about, even if you make a mistake. Suppose *you* do your best and *you* still make a mistake. Then you made a mistake. If you think, "I didn't do *my* best; somebody else did that best through me, and somebody else made the mistake," then you are not responsible for doing the best or doing the worst.

Literally speaking, none of us is doing anything here. There's only one doer: the Cosmic Intelligence that does everything and works through everybody. *That* is what put me here and is making me talk, and has put you there, and is making you listen—just because the show must go on. If we can understand this, life will be a super heaven for us. We will always be in bliss.

27 June

A DONKEY IS A DONKEY

Our first priority is to serve others. In the process of doing that, if you think that you have to take a little rest so that you can serve more, then go take rest. Still, your taking rest is for the purpose of serving. That's how you should eat, sleep, rest, bathe, everything. You take a bath with a nice soap not just to make yourself clean. You have to come here with a clean body so that you won't send out a bad odor to others. It is for the sake of others that you are keeping your body clean. It is to serve others that you eat your lunch. It is to serve others tomorrow that you go and rest tonight. We should think, "Everything I do is aimed towards serving others, my *all* is for others." If we can apply this in our daily lives then we don't have to worry about taking care of ourselves. Each one is already taken care of by everyone else.

Even being overly enthusiastic in wanting to serve more is the wrong approach. That's egoism. You should simply serve in whatever way you can. Don't try to show off. Don't pretend that you can do more than you are able to. A parrot can talk to you, but not a donkey. Does the donkey get upset over it? No. It's happy as a donkey. It need not try to copy the parrot and then cry, "Oh, I can't even sing or repeat anything." If you have been created as a donkey, be happy as a donkey, because you have a purpose. If you have been made something else, be happy that way.

28 June

THEN YOU WILL REALIZE YOUR OWN TRUE NATURE

Know that you are already liberated. You are never bound. Thinking that you are bound is ignorance. As the pure Self, you are never bound. The true Self is eternally pure, unchanging, immortal, never tainted by anything. It is always peaceful. But you don't see your true Self; you see the image of your true Self on the mirror of the mind. So when the mind gets tossed, the image is disturbed. The image seems to be assuming qualities because of the mind. The image seems to be bound. So you look at the image and say, "See, I'm bound." But in truth, *you* are never bound. If you still feel that you have to liberate yourself, the only liberation to be achieved is to liberate the mind from the selfishness that creates all these disturbances in the mind. Liberate yourself from the personal ego, the "I-ness," and the "my-ness,": "I want all those things. I must have everything." Liberate yourself from this. Then you will be always peaceful; you will realize the true nature of your own Self.

29 June

YOU CAN HEAR HIM WHISPERING

Certainly if you have that kind of faith and devotion, God can speak to you. You can hear Him whispering. There's nothing strange about it. But you must make sure of one thing. God is not the only one that speaks to you. There's some other fellow inside who also whispers to you. That fellow is your own ego. You can hear the voice of your own ego. Then, of course, you would ask, "How can I distinguish between them?" There is a testing stone for that. When God tells you something it is for your benefit as well as for everyone else's benefit. Nobody gets hurt when God asks you to do something. It's good for all. But if your ego says something, there is always something sneaky about it. There is a tinge of selfishness. *You* have to get something first, "Don't worry about others. Get it!" Yes. So, that is the testing stone. "Is it selfish or selfless? Is it for everybody's benefit or will someone get hurt by it?" If it would hurt somebody, God would never say that to you. God loves everyone equally. He's not interested in hurting someone else to make you happy. Remember that.

God also speaks to you through your own conscience. The conscience in you, in me, and in the other person will never differ because they are all from the same God. That's why sometimes when you do not know which voice is correct, you can go to somebody who you think is following God's advice within. But before you do that make sure that that person follows the true guidance of God in his life.

YOU ENJOY THE WHITE WRITING BECAUSE THERE IS A BLACK BOARD BEHIND IT

Don't give room for temporary depressions. Things come and go. Nothing is permanent in this world. Even our bodies come and go. You once had a young body; now you have an adult body. Someday you will have an old body, and one day you will even have a dead body. But still, you *have* a body. It's the body that goes through all these changes. *You* are immortal. Identify with that real you, the real "I."

When you play soccer, you kick the ball around. The ball goes through all the motions, but *you* are doing the playing. You enjoy the movements of the ball. Likewise, let your mind be your soccer ball. Wherever it goes, just enjoy it.

Even to enjoy nice, beautiful writing on a board, the board should be black because the chalk is white. You enjoy the white writing because there is a black board behind it. Don't forget that. You enjoy the pain because there is pleasure behind it.

We are the knowers, we are the seers. Remember that truth always. Apply this whenever you are in a depressed state. Jump up, shake it off and say, "Hey, I am a lion! This is all just temporary. I have come across this before and I know it will go away." You can heal yourself. There is a beautiful part of the mind, a powerful part of the mind, that can always get you out of any problem. Use that part, the brilliant part, the bright part. Don't succumb to the other side of the mind.

July

1 July

LIVE LIKE A LOTUS IN THE WATER

The lotus is considered to be a very holy and divine flower. Not just because of its beauty, but also because of its qualities. A lotus flower grows in very shallow water, usually in a muddy area. Though it comes out of the mud and mire, it rises as a beautiful flower that lives in the water without being affected by it. The lotus flower is always given as an example for one who wants to live spiritually in the world. It is said, "Live like a lotus in the water." The lotus leaf is right in the water, but it's never moistened by the water. When you pick it up, it's completely dry. It never gets wet. If you throw a little water over it, the water will roll off and scatter around like pearls.

A person should live like the lotus, being in the world but not affected by it. You should always express your natural beauty, though you may grow in a dirty place. Nothing from outside should affect you.

The lotus is a symbol of love and devotion also. If you ever see the Goddesses Lakshmi or Saraswati you would see that they're standing on a lotus. Wherever Lord Buddha placed his foot, a lotus appeared to hold it. The feet of a holy person are called the "lotus feet."

The lotus flower turns its head towards the sun always. That means it always turns towards the light; it receives the light constantly. So you can say it's an ever-enlightened flower.

2 July

BUT DID THEY BRING US LIBERTY?

Ultimately, we are all looking for happiness, and that cannot be experienced without liberty. We see happiness as God. Everything and everybody is looking for happiness. But it is not something that has to be brought in from outside. Happiness is already within us, and is to be experienced. No one can bring us liberty, bring us happiness. The founding fathers made the Declaration of Independence, but did they bring us liberty? Did they bring us happiness? They could not. They could only guide us, as all the great men and women do. We have to follow that guidance. The Declaration is a beautiful expression of age-old religious truth. We are all made in God's image, says the Bible. If we want to experience that joy within, we have to liberate ourselves from our own self-made bondage.

Nobody on earth is interested in binding you. Even if someone were interested, nobody *could* do that. It's completely in your hands to be bound or to be free. Bondage is not real. If you think that you are bound, you are bound. If you think that you are free right this moment, and that from time immemorial you have never been bound, then you *are* free. You feel that freedom. So, the freedom or the joy of freedom has to come from right thinking—from not thinking that you are bound. Who is a free person? The one who is interested in liberating himself or herself from self-made bondage.

3 July

HOIST YOUR FLAG

In a way the founding fathers wanted the entire America to be a Yogaville. That's what their intention was. And of course the founding fathers *here* wanted that. The founding sages and saints of all the great religions wanted this kind of freedom and independence or liberation throughout the universe. They didn't even bother to say, "Let Americans be free," but, "Let *all* be free. Let everyone and everything enjoy freedom." But of course if we can't think in those terms, at least let us think small to begin with and then keep expanding. That's what we are trying to achieve here.

Every individual is a Yogaville. You have problems within you. You have to have board meetings within you. All the outside meetings are ultimately to happen within. Just as the board people sit and analyze, analyze your own problems. For that sake your energy should really fly high. That is why the first and foremost thing is to hoist the flag. The flag is nothing but the *kundalini* or the sum total of consciousness within you rising up to the crown *chakra* at the top of the head. It should flutter there. You awaken the *kundalini* and let it unfurl and rise through your flagpost which is the spinal column. The string that you draw to raise the flag is your breath. One string comes down, one goes up: the incoming and outgoing breath. Lift up your energies. You cannot analyze and find the solution when your energies are low.

4 July

ON THIS SPECIAL DAY, MAKE A RESOLUTION

You all want to fly high. You want independence, liberty, happiness, but you don't want to do anything to get it. At least on a day like this you should reaffirm your interest in your practices and know that nobody has ever achieved anything without practice. Selfless service is all right. But even to do the service correctly, with the proper attitude, with proper physical energy, you have to tune up your body and mind. If the battery is weak, your quartz clock won't run. You have to charge your battery. That's where the personal practices come in. Snatch a little bit of time somehow to wind your clock, and then throughout the day you can unwind. It seems to be the other way around. In your activities, you get wound up. You should be unwinding. Make a new resolution that, "Yes, I am going to let my flag fly. Let it rise up my flagpost, through my practices." Keep the post straight by the yoga postures. Pull the strings by proper breathing. Raise the flag of consciousness. Then you won't have to do anything else. The result will be there.

On this beautiful day my sincere wish and prayer is that all of you will really put your effort into experiencing this joy of liberty.

5 July

WE RECEIVE ACCORDING TO OUR TUNING

All the thoughts that the entire world is thinking and will think and has thought before are already in the cosmic mind. They are there waiting for you to draw upon. By thinking of something, you literally become a sort of receiving set. All of the similar thoughts come to you. It's not that you create anything new. Actually, there is nothing new; nothing can be created and nothing can be destroyed. Nobody has ever "created" any new thinking. We are receiving constantly. And we receive according to our tuning. The music is there, but if you tune to the wrong station you will get atmospheric disturbance. Both are there. You call it "disturbance" because you don't want it, but it is there. The music also is there. So we simply tune to receive. Sometimes even without your conscious effort, the tuner of your receiving set seems to be in a certain location; all of a sudden it receives and then you say, "Oh, I am experiencing something new. I never thought of that before." It just comes to you, even without your conscious effort, because the mind simply rolls to that frequency and happens to receive it. Your mind is nothing but a part of the cosmic mind, and a part of the cosmic mind is functioning through you.

6 July

YOU ARE NOT AFRAID OF ANYTHING

It's not possible to give a common answer for all the different kinds of fears. But the basic reason for fear is the lack of knowledge of our true Self, which is imperishable, immortal. If that is realized, there is no fear of death. And once you get over the fear of death, you are not afraid of anything.

YOU SHOULD BE HAPPY ABOUT THAT

If everything that comes from outside—money, friends, family, name, fame — were going to make you happy, there wouldn't be any need for churches, synagogues, spiritual centers or religions. Nobody would need to read the Bible. Why? You would be happy with your money, you would be happy with your friends. Why would you need anything else? Therefore, all these things should make you unhappy. I'm sorry, it's a little hard-hearted to say this. Everything must ultimately cheat you and deceive you, and hit you so hard that you turn back to God. And that's what will happen to a sincere seeker. That's God's Will.

In a way, when people are not ready to realize God, they will even be tempted to go out and chase things. And they will be given that piecemeal happiness here and there. When people find real pleasure in the world outside, it shows that God is not in a hurry to get them. It's true. If God is in a hurry to get you, He will make you displeased with everything outside very soon. If you look at the life history of the saints, you will find that the minute they became God-conscious they got into all kinds of problems, suffering after suffering, suffering after suffering. Why? God says, "Ahh, you wanted me, you should come quickly to me, so I will make everybody hit you so that you come to me soon." So don't feel bad if it happens to you. You should be happy about that.

8 July

AT LEAST SAY A NICE WORD

The great saintly poet, Subramuniya Bharati, once said, "Come on, all you people. Let us build a temple. All those who have plenty of money, bring heaps of dollars. Heaps of gold. Those who have little money, bring pennies. And those who do not even have pennies, at least say a nice word." Not everyone can afford to give hundreds and thousands of dollars. If you cannot give even a penny, don't sit there and say something negative, "Ahh, it's all nonsense." Even by not saying anything negative, you can contribute to something.

YOU OBSERVE THE DAY AND YOU RECEIVE THE BENEFIT

Only a candle that is lit and shining can give a little light to the other candles. If you simply sit there as an unlit candle and listen to hours and hours and hours of talk about light, you won't get lit. You have to come, touch the lamp, and get a spark before you get lit. That is the duty of a disciple. After having seen a lit candle, you should go, bow down and then get the touch. Once you have gotten that, you work on yourself, make your life brighter. Of course, since you remember that you got the light from another lamp, you are grateful to that light. This is why we dedicate a special day each year in honor of all the great masters, sages and saints. They were flaming torches. We touch them in some form or other and get a little spark. We humble ourselves in front of those great sages and saints and express our gratitude, and by doing that we are able to receive more. We give our gratitude to our mothers on Mother's Day and our fathers on Father's Day. In the same way we give our gratitude to the spiritual teacher, or the guru, who ultimately helps us to realize the final goal: the Truth, or God, or the inner Light.

So Guru Poornima Day, or All Prophets Day, is not just a mere celebration. It is an observance. You observe the day, and you receive the benefit. May the blessings of all the great sages and saints and masters be upon you all to make your life more shining, more peaceful, more healthy and more happy. May you in turn share those blessings with all other beings so that one day we can see a beautiful blessed heaven on this earth.

NOTHING IS IMPOSSIBLE

Question: There are times when illnesses aren't relieved by treatment. Do we have illness for a period of time because it's our karma? If so, how do we know when that period is over?

Sri Gurudev: When your illness is over, you know that the karma period is over. If it persists you should know that the karma is still there. That's simple, is it not? But don't always blame karma. Karma is not something that somebody gave you. Nobody creates karma for you. You have the capacity to erase it and purge it out. Have this idea well rooted in your system: "It's my karma. I acquired it, and I can remove it. I can be done with that. Nobody else is the cause for my karma." Then you can comfortably work on it. Here the challenge comes. Which one is greater? The karma, or you? If you put forth more energy than your karma, certainly you can overcome it. But if your energy is not enough, the karma seems to win. Still, it has its own time period. After having given its reward to you, whether pleasurable or painful, it gets purged out and ceases. So have confidence and continue to work on it.

In the case of ill health think about it. What did you do to affect your health? Make the necessary changes. It takes a long time. If it has taken years to get into such a condition, you can't expect to correct the problem in days.

Take your time and be patient. Nothing is impossible. You can heal yourself because *you* created your disease. Now, you can create your health. You are the master of it. Never give up. Fast. Change your diet. Pray. The best form of healing is prayer. The physical treatment is not enough. Have a happy and contented mind. The best remedy for any illness is laughter.

11 July

YOU ARE ALREADY MARRIED TO YOUR PEACE AND JOY

Relationships need not be difficult. If you don't have any selfish purpose, then you don't expect anything and you don't lose anything. You are just there together. When you are apart, you are apart. You aren't attached to that relationship.

Realize that you don't have to have a relationship to be happy. You are already married to your peace and joy. When you are married, things outside look more inviting. Right at home you have the prettiest girl, the most handsome fellow, but you don't appreciate that. It's natural. So God says, "All right, if you want to have that, okay, go, try to be happy." But when you get tired of all that, then you say, "Oh, no, no, no, no, I don't think I'll ever by happy with any of those things." Then God says, "All right, then live with me." It's true. That means you don't realize your own true nature, which is happiness. The minute you realize that you are always happy, that you are always peaceful whether you have a relationship or not, that you have a permanent relationship within, then you no longer worry about an outside relationship. If it comes, fine, if it doesn't come, wonderful. You become independent. You don't depend on anything or anyone for your happiness.

12 July

TRAIN YOUR EYES TO SEE THE BRIGHT SIDE OF EVERYTHING

"As you think, so you become." Think well, you will be well. Think ill, you will be ill. It's all your thought. Sometimes you might not be thinking ill of yourself, but you are thinking ill of others. That is still thinking ill. Whether it is about you or somebody else, that is what you are thinking. When you think of that, you will become that. That is why we say, "See no evil, hear no evil, speak no evil." If you see evil, hear evil, speak evil, you will become evil. It's not to save others that you are asked not to think ill, not to speak ill. You will not be hurting them, but you will be hurting yourself. In our lives we should always think well. Train your eyes to see the bright side of everything.

13 July

A PERFECT ACT

No action is undesirable as long as it produces a beneficial result to all concerned, including you. You may call that a perfect act. The definition of a perfect act is one that neither hurts you, nor hurts anyone else. At the same time, it should bring at least some benefit to somebody. Sometimes due to past life experiences, or lack of proper training, the mind would want to do things that are not beneficial. Gently direct the mind, educate it. That is yoga. The very purpose of all your spiritual practice is to learn how to direct your thoughts and actions for a good purpose.

YOU CAN DO IT, YOU CAN UNDO IT, AND YOU CAN DO IT DIFFERENTLY

Your upbringing certainly has a say over your temperament; but as you grow, your true temperament will come to the surface more. You will be urged to do something—possibly something very different.

When your true temperament comes out, then you will know that's the real you. Sit and question yourself, "What is it that I am naturally interested in?" The Bhagavad Gita calls it *swadharma*—the natural tendency or natural temperament. Sometimes you might come across a sort of natural temperament that is not fit for your growth. You might have been developing in the wrong way before. But remember, even your natural temperament was not given to you by someone else. It's yours. You made it before, and you brought it with you. Now, after learning and studying and knowing a little bit more, you might think, "That's not the right temperament for me to develop; that may be what I came with, but it's not conducive anymore, so I'm going to change it." That's where you exercise your mastery.

If you are strong enough, you can brush it all aside completely and open up a new chapter in your life. You are the master of your destiny. You can do it, you can undo it, and you can do it differently. Don't ever, ever blame your environment on somebody else: "Oh, my Dad used to do this, my Mom used to do this, so I am like this." They probably did it because that's what they knew. You don't have to be influenced by that.

Always use your temperament in doing something beautiful, something beneficial for the entire humanity. It should not be limited only to you or your family or a small group. Think big. Always. That is why we pray, "May *all* be happy." When you say *all* automatically a little part of you is also included in that.

15 July

WHEREVER PEOPLE GLORIFY A THING, I AM THERE

Question: The Bible talks about "false gods." What is a false god?

Sri Gurudev: If God is omnipresent, what could be called a false God? God is present in name, in fame, in money. The Bhagavad Gita says wherever people glorify a thing, I am there. What would be a false God then? Anything that you don't see as the expression of God. The falsehood is in your approach. In the way you look at things. If you see everything as the expression of God, it's all God. That is the difference between real God and false God. God is everywhere, but often we forget that.

What makes it a false God? It's not somebody else worshipping God in some other form that makes it a false God to you. When you don't see God in something, it becomes a false God then. It's still God's manifestation, but because of superficial things you don't see it that way. Then it becomes a false God to you. People should see everything as God's expression; they should worship, adore, love, respect, and approach it that way.

16 July

IN A WAY EVERYTHING IS SELFISH, NO DOUBT

Selfishness is when you feel, "I *must* have it at any cost." Use your discriminating faculty. Analyze your motives." Why am I selfish? What am I gaining out of that?" By being selfish, you are not going to be happy at all. Selfishness makes you miserable. Any time you are unhappy, if you look for the cause, you will see that you were selfish in doing things, in your approach, or in your thinking. That's why a selfish person can never, never, never be happy.

In a way everything is selfish, no doubt. Even wanting to be peaceful at all times is selfish. You want peace and health so that you can grow spiritually; it sounds selfish. But that kind of selfishness is not wrong. If you find the peace in you, people all around you will be benefited by your peaceful nature. Even if you don't consciously do anything for them or say anything to them, you will be setting an example, and they will learn from your example. So that is a sort of selfless selfishness.

EVERY MORNING YOU HAVE TWO, THREE DEITIES TO DECORATE

Question: I believe in the teachings, and try to apply them, but I am not very regular in the formal practices. This causes me pain. Should I make more of an effort to do formal *sadhana* or should I consider the pain to be a part of my spiritual practice?

Sri Gurudev: Well, it is part of your *sadhana.* Almost all the devotees of God felt the pain of not doing enough to reach Him. That pain is a helpful thing. It reminds you of where you are. If you don't feel bad about it, if you just say, "Okay, Swamiji said to take it easy, if I don't meditate it doesn't matter," then you will not grow. When you are not doing the right thing, you should really feel pain. That will help you to change.

At the same time, you should know your situation in life. If you are a wife and the mother of three children, you have certain family responsibilities also. If for that reason you cannot follow all the disciplines, getting up at a certain time and meditating for an hour and doing everything, you should not feel bad; but if you are not practicing due to your laziness, then you should feel hurt. If your responsibilities don't allow you to do everything you are excused for that, because you still have your first and foremost responsibility as a wife and a mother. You have to take care of the children. That is also part of yoga. So you should ask yourself, "Am I not following everything due to my laziness, or due to my other responsibilities?" Then make the other responsibilities part of your practice also. For example, if you are all alone as an individual you may clean your altar and shrine room and decorate everything and sit and meditate. But as a mother every morning you have two, three deities to decorate. Pull them out of the bed, wash them, give them a nice bath, dress them well, feed them. That is the offering that you are giving to God. They are living gods in your home until you see them off to school. If you ignore them and go and sit and close your eyes and meditate, then God says, "What is this? You offer a piece of fruit on the altar, but I am here in your home in the form of your child and you ignore me."

18 July

WELL-EARNED MONEY WILL NEVER BE ROBBED

If ever you lose money all of a sudden, know that it was ill-earned money. Well-earned money will never be robbed. I'll give you a small illustration.

Once upon a time in a village there lived a milkman who had a few cows. He used to milk them, and take the milk to the next village where he sold it to the restaurant owners. Slowly, slowly he became greedy and started adding water to the milk. Eventually, he doubled the quantity. If he got a gallon of milk, he added a gallon of water, and sold it as two gallons of milk. He did that for a long time.

One day, on his way home, it started raining. He had to cross a river, but the river was in flood. So he tied all the money he had saved—a thousand dollars—into a bundle, and slowly started out across the river. When he was halfway across, he fell into the water. He was a good swimmer, however, and somehow swam to the other shore. As soon as he came out of the water, he checked his money; the bundle was there, but it was all disturbed. He wanted to make sure all the money was still there, so he started counting it. There was only five hundred dollars; he had lost five hundred. And he sat down and cried.

A wise man came by and asked the milkman what was wrong; after hearing what had happened, he said, "Well, you are a milkman aren't you?" "Yes, yes, I am." "Don't worry, you still have your milk money. The water money went with the water. The milk money came with you. Every time you cross the river, you pour a gallon of water into your milk. You took the water from the river, so the river took that five hundred dollars."

There is a village proverb, "Milk money is in the milk. Water money is in the water." Remember that always. It's not how much you earn, but *how* you earn it, that's important. Your money should be very honest, clean money. Then you will always be benefited by it.

19 July

A LITTLE HEAVEN ON THE EARTH

Question: At Satchidananda Ashram-Yogaville, which is based on your teachings, there is a temple called the Light Of Truth Universal Shrine [LOTUS]. What is your vision for the temple and the ashram?

Sri Gurudev:

My vision of LOTUS and Yogaville is a village filled with people who follow the yogic principles. Everything that is conducive to the yoga philosophy and lifestyle will be seen there. That's my vision. In plain, simple language, my vision is for Yogaville to be a little heaven on earth.

Every village should have a temple; first you build the temple, and then you live around it. So the LOTUS is a part of Yogaville. We are putting God in the center, and building everything else around Him. LOTUS is religious yoga. Yogaville is practical yoga. The purpose of the LOTUS is to bring the religions together. The purpose of Yogaville is to bring people together. That's why the LOTUS is part of Yogaville. In Yogaville we can live as a good community of yogis according to the yogic principles. The outside world may not know much about it, until and unless they come and see what is happening. But the LOTUS will draw outside attention also. It's something unique and it will create an interest in us and our work. Here we are putting all the world religions under one roof. In that respect, it is unique. It should be the pride of Yogaville. Our goal is to make a beautiful Yogaville community and to prove to the world that as yogis we can live healthily, happily. We can live with all ease and with all peace, and be of good use.

20 July

THE BEST CHARITY

There is only one Light Of Truth Universal Shrine now, a place like this where people of all faiths and beliefs can come together and silently worship in their own way under the same roof. But this is only a beginning. I know that once people see the beauty and benefit of understanding among all religions, every town will want a LOTUS. I'm sure that will happen.

It's not just something for only a few people to experience; everyone should be able to participate. But somewhere, somebody has to begin. Probably God has chosen us as instruments to do that. So our aim is to educate people not to fight in the name of religion, but to experience their spiritual oneness.

Let us know that we are all one in spirit; essentially, we are one appearing as many. The moment that kind of understanding comes, almost all other problems, both physical and material, will be solved. Until then they will never be solved.

Anything that is done to bring this knowledge to people is the greatest deed. Any charity that's used for this purpose is the best form of charity. I don't deny the other charities; they are doing much great work. But if we work toward real universal love and understanding we are going to the very root of the other problems. Achieving this should be first and foremost. Once we eliminate the cause of hunger, poverty, all the other problems, we will no longer have to worry about solving them.

Do what you can for this cause; I'm not speaking just about the LOTUS, but about the cause of spiritual understanding. Learn to care and share, to love and give, and inspire others by your example. Spread these ideas. Then you are carrying a LOTUS with you in your heart.

21 July

YOU ARE ALWAYS DOING SPIRITUAL WORK

You are always doing spiritual work. To know whether you are doing it properly, watch your feelings. Are you becoming more and more easeful? More and more peaceful? Are you lessening your worries? Do you always feel happy? If it bothers you more and more, then you are not doing it right. It's not the action that is important, but how you do it.

To decide whether you are doing the work in a spiritual way or not, ask yourself: "Am I maintaining my peace while doing this?" If the answer is "No," then you are doing something wrong. Every job should make you happy, jubilant. You should enjoy it, whatever it is, and feel like doing more. You should forget yourself while you are doing it. Work should be fun, not a burden. If you become heavy while doing it, then you are doing it as a labor. Even if you look for a thank you, you are looking for some reward. When you do something for a reward, it's labor. It's not service. Labor means you do it to get it. Service means you just do it, and forget it.

22 July

THE PRAYER WILL COME

Question: Could you suggest a prayer that a sick person might say?

Sri Gurudev: There's no need for a suggestion. If he or she is really sick, the prayer will come. You don't need to worry about the words. God will know what you mean. And remember, a really hearty cry relieves a lot of psychological problems. Don't ever be ashamed of crying. I remember a South Indian saint used to say, "Lord, I know the trick. I know how to get You. If I cry, You cannot resist. If I cry, I'll get You; but my ego never allows me to cry."

23 July

WHO CONTROLS THE PLANETS?

Astrology is also controlled by your karma. Why were you born at a certain time, in a certain place, under certain stars? Because it was your karma. So your astrological chart itself is a product of your karma. If you have good karma, you will be reborn on an auspicious day. Why is it that you were born as a Cancer, as a Libra, as a Gemini? *You* chose stars. You chose a time. Some of you might say, "No. My doctor chose the time," but actually you made the doctor choose. Ultimately, it's all your own doing.

By changing your karma, you can change your horoscope. Maybe because of your past karma you have given room for some of the planets to control you. By developing a stronger karma, you can change that; you can make it null and void. Then Saturn cannot affect you; Jupiter and Mars cannot affect you. You can command them. Astrology is completely powerless in front of your karma. You have the capacity to command your stars to move around.

A great saint used to say, "When I have the vision of the Lord always, what can these planets do to me? They have no power to affect me because I have taken refuge in the Lord." Who controls the planets? Who controls time? Who controls space? When you become the beloved of that Lord, all of His servants will be ready to obey you.

24 July

SUCH A MARRIAGE WILL LAST

The one and only thing that will keep a marriage going is to think: "God has brought me a partner. No matter what he or she is, I am learning to serve that person unconditionally. It is for that reason I am marrying someone, not for anything else." He or she may seem to be nice, wonderful, an angel, but within a month you will see the ego coming out. Certainly it is going to be difficult then. If you are getting into a matrimonial relationship with someone, know that you are having somebody to offer all your services to. Don't expect anything in return from that person. Both of you should think that way. Such a marriage will last.

25 July

NEVER FORGET WHAT YOU GOT THAT IS GOOD

If you really want to develop more faith and devotion, then think about the great benefits and gifts you have been constantly receiving. The more you think of them, the more you feel grateful, the more you feel devoted, the more you feel love. But unfortunately, our tendency is to forget all the nice gifts, and instead to remember the one small thing that we did not get. Never forget what you received that is good, even though it is small; but don't even remember it for a minute if somebody has done some harm to you. Even this one teaching is enough to help us to see friends, and friends, and only friends, everywhere. And that's how you develop your devotion.

YOU HAVE A GREAT TASK, AND IT'S NOT IMPOSSIBLE

Why are we seeing so many psychological cases now? Why are even the children becoming neurotic? What's happening to the world? Somehow in the name of civilization and culture, we have lost our strength. We have lost control over our own senses. We have become weak. That's why nowadays nobody even wants to make a commitment. The minute you get married, the commitment chokes you. You immediately feel, "Ohh, it's too much for me, I can't live like this." You want to get out. There is no commitment between husband and wife, between parents and child, between teacher and student, between employer and employee.

Commitment is very important in life. Those who want to lead a spiritual life are here to change all these things and to rebuild a better world. Remember that. You have a great task, and it's not impossible. If you really put your heart and soul into that, you can do it. Begin with your own life. Let nothing shake you. You have to be really bold and strong to achieve anything in life. Be that bold. When you know that something is right, don't hesitate to follow it. Certainly there may be obstacles, tests; but don't give up. Even if you should fall down or make a mistake, get up and say, "No! The next time I'll be strong." Keep on going, like great mountain climbers, until you reach the top. If you really want to do it, you will be given the needed strength. You will have all the support. If you want it, you've got it; but your want has to be that strong.

27 July

EVERYTHING IS GOD'S WORK

Somehow my life has been continuously directed by a Higher Will. I didn't have any interest in coming to this country. I didn't have any interest in going to Sri Lanka. Somehow, Providence put me in various places. It just pushed me here, there, here, there, one place after the other. As if some unseen hand were moving me, even from childhood itself. I never *wanted* to do anything myself. I simply accepted whatever was presented to me. After high school I went to study some technical things. When I finished that and came back, I was immediately asked to go manage a temple. From the temple management, I was pushed into the automobile field. It all just happened. Somebody called me, "Come, you do this." Whatever came, I accepted. "Yes, maybe I have something to learn there." Even going to different teachers was like that. It's not that it was *my* wish. From the very beginning, there was some hand behind everything, guiding me from place to place. And that hand is still functioning. I am here today. I don't know where I will be tomorrow. I'm ever ready to move according to the Will of that Higher Force, and that is enough for me. That keeps me always peaceful, contented, happy and carefree. That's what you call renunciation. Renounce your personal interest and the Lord will work through you. He will put you wherever it's necessary. Whatever is presented to you, do it happily, joyfully. Everything is God's work.

28 July

THE WHOLE OF LIFE IS SHOW BUSINESS

Question: Is it possible to develop spiritually while working in a highly competitive and hectic field such as show business?

Sri Gurudev: We call it show business. Why? Do you think that show business is to show somebody else something? No. Show business is to show *you* something: yourself. It will teach you about the worth and the worthlessness of things in life. Yes. Show business means it's all just made up. It's all superficial. And when you learn that lesson, then you can use that same philosophy in your life. The whole of life is show business. What am I doing here? I'm acting my part. What are you doing there? You're acting your part. We're having a show. There is no superior and inferior cast in this. We are all needed to make the show. You have taken a part, so play it well. We are all one in spirit, but I am playing the part of the teacher today. You are playing the part of being a little ignorant. Behave that way. Don't get up and say, "I know more than you;" the show will collapse. When the curtain falls, we are all one and the same.

The whole world is superficial; it's constantly, constantly changing. Our relationships change, our situations change, our positions change, our names change. I was a baby, then I became a young boy, then an adult, then an old man. Changes, changes, changes. So what is the reality? The spiritual truth. We are all essentially one. That never changes. Where can you learn this truth faster than in show business?

29 July

IF YOU CAN, DO SOMETHING

Simply take it easy, trust in God, and do what you can. Let whatever you do be for the benefit of others. If you can, do something. If you cannot, accept it. Somebody else will do it; it is not that you have to do it all yourself. Honestly try to do your part, but know that you are not the end–all. You are not going to do everything. If a thing is meant to happen, it will happen. Just begin. Start it and if it has to happen through you, more energy will come to you. If not, you will very soon know that you are not to do that. Accept it. Do your best, and leave the rest.

30 July

THE REAL ME IS THE SPIRIT

Question: Swamiji, I have loved you for a long time. How much longer will it be till I get closer to you and to enlightenment?

Sri Gurudev: Ohhh, my sweetheart. If you have really loved the real Swamiji you are already closer to him. He is closer than your own heart. That is the real Swamiji you should love. Don't think that Swamiji is this physical person sitting here. No. The spirit in *you* is the real Swamiji. I am only a mirror to reflect that in you. If you learn to see *that* Swamiji, that guru in you, then you are never apart from that. And you are already enlightened. As long as you think that the guru or the Swamiji is somewhere sitting outside in a physical form, then this kind of separation and distance is there, and that will not bring enlightenment. You should see the light of wisdom that is in every heart. It's not the monopoly of a few people. Ultimately you have to turn within. You say, "I have loved you for a long time." Why? Is it because I have a long beard? Is it because I sit and talk nicely, sometimes make you laugh? Is it because people call me the Founder/Director of a big institute or this or that? No. That's not the real me. That's all temporary. It won't stay long. But the real me is the spirit. Or, if you like, certain qualities that you might admire in me. *That* is the guru. If you admire those qualities in me, develop those qualities in you, then you will really feel close to the Swamiji in you.

31 July

WHEN YOU SEE YOUR NEIGHBOR, MELT THE SAME WAY

Question: At times my surrender is quite intense and I feel that I am melting at the mention of God's name. Can you offer any advice to develop pure love and the higher states of Divine Love?

Sri Gurudev: When pure love matures, it will take you to the higher state itself. You don't have to worry about higher states. "Melting at the mention of God's name" itself is enough. Slowly it will lead you to further and further experiences, in a natural way. When you see your neighbor, melt in the same way. That's even more important. When you see your pets, melt in that way. When you see your plants, melt in that way. Not only when you hear God's name. Try to apply this love toward everything around you.

August

1 August

YOU WOULD EVEN ENJOY HELL

Wherever you go, you carry your own imagination. Even if you go to heaven, you won't be able to see it as heaven if there is a hell in your heart. If you have a heaven in your heart, you would even enjoy hell. Yes, it's true. Because you would see heaven there. It's all up to you.

2 August

YOU CAN ENJOY THE SAME

For one month live a totally surrendered life. Try that life for a while. For a sample week, or a sample month. Just say, "Let God take care of me. And let me do my duty. Whatever God has given me to do, let me fulfill it." That means wherever you are, God has placed you there. He has given you some job, you are doing it. I don't say that you should not have ambition. Have the biggest ambition. What is the biggest ambition? To maintain your peace. Yes. Let that be your ambition. "I have to maintain my peace at all costs. I am ready to give up anything and everything for the sake of peace." That's your biggest goal. And that's what you call God. Peace is your God. "For the sake of God, I am ready to renounce everything." That means God and Peace are one and the same. God and Happiness are one and the same.

I am simply telling you what I have been doing all these years. By following this truth, I am living a worryless life. There's nobody or nothing that can rob me of my peace and happiness. If you have a bigger goal, all right, go ahead and try it. But if you think this is your goal, then try it; I am sure you will enjoy that peace.

If you think that I am really happy and peaceful, there is no need to envy me. You can enjoy the same. It's not anybody's monopoly. Every one of you can enjoy this. God is our Father. He has not given nice things only to one person or two persons and not the other people. He has given this wealth to all equally. It's everybody's property. If we don't enjoy it, it's not His fault.

3 August

PRAYER ALSO IS A SORT OF NOVOCAINE

The dentist who administers novocaine is not taking away the pain. He or she is just temporarily keeping it away. Afterwards, you still feel the pain. In the same way, prayer also is a sort of novocaine. When you pray you feel comforted, but you still have to go through the operation. So the operation has to be performed, but it is done under a sort of reduced pain. All our prayers and even the prayers and blessings from others, the good wishes and get well cards, all help us to rise above the pain: "So many people are praying for me. So many people are thinking of me. I'm getting the blessings of so many people, so I'll get through it." That feeling itself reduces the pain. Because after all what is pain? It's in the mind. Pain is a sort of illusion. There's no pain at all as such. Suppose you have an abscess in your tooth. It pains a lot. Even when you go to bed, you can't sleep because it hurts so much. Then, when you really get tired, you slowly slip into sleep. Do you still feel the pain when you sleep? No. Does the abscess go away? No. The tooth is there, the abscess is there, but you don't feel the pain. The minute you are awake, then "Oh, oh, oh, oh, oh!" The pain comes again. So where is the pain? If the pain is in the tooth, the pain should continue until the tooth is healed. But, instead, when the mind forgets the tooth and the abscess, there's no pain. When the mind thinks of it, the pain comes back. Is it not so?

Do you know the treatment for a scorpion sting? The treatment is to put a drop of salt water in the eye. The sting in the eye is much greater than the sting in the hand, so the pain in the hand is forgotten and the mind is diverted to the pain in the eye. Of course, after a little while the tears flush out the eye, and that pain goes away. Because you have forgotten this pain due to that pain, and because that pain went away, you don't go back to this pain.

It is the same way with your prayers also. In a way, they nullify your pain. But the problem is still there. It has to be taken care of. We have to do whatever is necessary.

ACCEPT IT AND SEEK HELP

Illness can be karmic; the reaction to your past actions. The best way to deal with that is to know that it is your past karma that has brought this. Pray sincerely, "Lord, let me accept this and do whatever I can to clean it up." It does not mean that you should not seek help from others. Accept the illness *and* seek help. The mere acceptance will take away half the pain of the illness. The illness becomes painful when you deny it, when you don't want it. So, accepting the karmic reaction is an important thing. But sometimes people don't have the proper understanding and they say, "Oh, it's my karma. What can *I* do about it?" That is wrong. You do what you can.

5 August

LIKE A LOTUS FLOWER IN THE WATER

There is a simple way of finding out how far away you are from God. Take a pencil and paper, and start writing down all the things that you call "mine." However long the list is, that's how far away you are from God. Reduce the list, and you are coming closer to God. If there is nothing to call "mine," you are God. Remember, when you say that so many things are "mine, mine, mine, mine" you have literally thrown mines all around you. They are ready to explode at any moment. You cannot even walk with ease.

It's not that you are asked to throw everything away and ignore your responsibilities. Keep them there, but don't label them as "mine." Label them as "Thine." "God, I am Thine. All is Thine. Thy will be done." That way you are possessing the whole world, but the world is not going to possess you. You will be like the lotus flower in the water; untouched, untainted by the world around you.

6 August

WE ARE ALL MARRIED TO ONE ANOTHER IN SPIRIT

We are all related to each other. We are all united. All we have to do is understand that and experience it. We are related in spirit. That is the only relationship we have, and nobody can break it. Even if two people want to break it, they cannot. All other relationships are something other than the spiritual relationship. And those relationships will always change, because they are based on changing things. When two individuals come together under a matrimonial tie, that's what you call a marital relationship. What is it that they are marrying? The true marriage is already there. It was performed already in heaven. We are all married to one another in spirit.

AT A CERTAIN LEVEL YOU ARE ABLE TO SEE BOTH SIDES

Question: Everything comes from God, and thus everything is God. Therefore, how can it be said that there is a true Self and not true Self; or that, "I am not the body, not the mind." It is like saying, "God is everything except the body, mind, etc."

Sri Gurudev: Very true. When you know that everything is God, and when you are experiencing everything as God, then you don't even say, "I am not the body, I am not the mind." The fellow who says, "I am not the body, not the mind," is not experiencing everything as God. So there are different levels. When you are at the lower level you say, "This is Self and this is non-Self." The duality comes. That's how you begin. But as you go further and further, everything becomes the Self, including body and mind, right and wrong. There is no wrong then. Even the so-called "wrong" is also right.

In one of his prayers the great sage Acharya Shankara praises God in this way. There is a Hindu form of worship called *archana* in which you offer flowers and repeat the name of God and His attributes. At one point he says, "O Lord, in the form of anger, my salutations to You. O Lord, in the form of lust, I am saluting You." How could that be? One should not have lust. At the same time he is saying, "God, in the form of lust, my salutations to You." It looks like a contradiction, does it not? It is not a contradiction if you put them all on the same level. On one level even lust becomes God. But at another level, when you don't know how to use it, it becomes a terrible thing. When you don't understand it, when you are looking at it in the wrong way, it becomes something undesirable. After all, there *is* only God. At a certain level you are able to see it from both sides. Then you see that they are one and the same. There's no difference at all. At that point you say, "O lust, my salutations. O jealousy, my salutations, because you're a quality of God. There's nothing other than God. Without God, nothing is possible." So it depends upon your level of growth. Both are correct at their levels. So we should not condemn any philosophy. People look at things from various sides. To them, it's right. If you put yourself in their position, you will know they are right. Allow them to continue that way.

WE ARE ALL SPIRITUAL BEINGS

Question: I am part of a women's group. Please advise us of any special chants or prayers or observances that will keep us aware of who we really are. We wish to unfold gracefully in accordance with spiritual teachings.

Sri Gurudev: Well, if you want to become aware of who you really are, don't even form men's groups and women's groups. Men's groups and women's groups are formed in terms of a bundle of flesh and bone. We have to rise above the physical level. We have to transcend the physical, and the mental also.

The spiritual state is a transcendental state. As long as we get caught in the body and mind, we are not going to recognize the spirit. So if you really want to know who you are, say, "I'm not a woman, I'm not a man. I'm not a scholar, I'm not a fool." Yes. All this scholarliness and foolishness are in the mind. So know that: "I am spirit originally, essentially, using the feminine body, so I am calling myself a woman." That's all. Because you have a little body, you call yourself a child. Because you have a wrinkled body, you call yourself old. So you are associating yourself with the body and mind. That is what creates all the problems. If we really want to know who we are, we must rise above all these things and say, "We are all spiritual beings. We are the image of God. We are all lights, burning, shining through different bulbs." Some are good old 110 volt. There are also 108 volt. The minute you forget that, you revolt. So keep up the voltage.

EVERY ACTION HAS A REACTION

Question: Do we incur bad karma each time we kill a bug or insect or frog while driving down the road?

Sri Gurudev: Yes. Whatever we do, knowingly or unknowingly, brings karma. There's no doubt about it. Even when you walk you might step on many insects.

What should we do about that? The scriptures have given certain solutions. In our own life, as far as possible, we can offer our energy—material or physical, whatever it is—for the benefit of others to annihilate these bad karmas. It is called *yagnya* or sacrifice. There is a difference between the conscious karma and the unconscious or unavoidable karma. You have to pay for any karma done consciously, it is true; but you also have to do something in order to survive. You cannot escape from that. There is unavoidable karma. The only way out is to feel, "All right, having killed this many things while eating, breathing, driving, and walking, let me offer my energy for the benefit of the creation." Pray; offer your service to others. That is *yagnya. Yagnya* means always offering back more than you receive.

People can be categorized into five groups. The thief, the debtor, the fair businessman, the good person and the saint. Who is a thief? The one who always gets things from everyone, but never gives anything. The debtor gets ten dollars worth but gives only five dollars worth to others. The fair businessman is the one who gets ten dollars worth of benefit from others and returns ten dollars worth. A good person gets ten dollars and gives at least twenty or thirty dollars—more than what he gets. And a saint doesn't get anything; he just gives everything he can. So you can analyze your own life and see in which category you belong. The only way to wash out our bad karma is to be a really good person or a saint. That means through our service to the earth, to the people, to divine beings, to God. That way we can be pardoned for the karmas that we incur unconsciously.

10 August

THE BEST VICTORY

So much discipline is necessary to fight a war, and that is only a simple war against our brothers. The war that spiritual seekers are trying to fight is against a bigger enemy. Unfortunately you cannot even see the enemy. Your enemy works through your eyes, through your nose, through your tongue, through every cell of your body. You are surrounded by the enemy. You need so much discipline to fight it. It's a continuous battle until you really win over the senses. Of course when you win over your enemies, they are no longer enemies, they become friends. That's the best victory. The real victory is not in killing the enemy, but in making him your friend.

THE CLOSEST FRIEND IS THE GOD WITHIN

To a real spiritual seeker, God is the only buddy. All the other friends are equal. There is no, "She is close to me," or "He is my best friend." Spiritual seekers don't form cliques. That's all in the mind. A spiritual person should be above these discriminations.

The closest friend is the One within. Your God, or your mantram. If you still want a closest friend in human form, then your teacher. Otherwise you are alone. You can have other associations, but watch for the result. Ask yourself, "Am I getting the benefit of becoming more rooted in my spiritual life? Is this association helping me, or is it shaking me? Is it creating more attachment and confusion?" We always have to think in those terms. "This is my path. I want to lead a detached life, a serviceful life. Not a personal life." So your friendships should not be personal friendships. Your friendship is because he or she happened to be here and you are working together. Yes, friends. But not *personal* friends. A renunciate doesn't have anything personal, because that person is already gone. The minute you put somebody or something as personal, attachment starts to come and that confuses the mind. So spiritual life is like that, not having anything as personal—whether you are a monk or a householder.

A householder can also live like that; then he is a renunciate in the house, that's all. There's no *personal* relationship, but we are duty-bound. "My position is this, 'Yes, I am the husband, I am the father of this house. I have a duty to perform to my wife, to my children, to take care of them. Other than that, I love everyone equally. Because I have some duty to the immediate family, I seem to be showing more love to them.'" But that doesn't mean that you are not showing your love to others. It's not your change of name or change of dress that makes you a renunciate. The lifestyle and mental attitude toward things and people makes you a renunciate.

GOD IS NEARER TO YOU THAN YOUR OWN HEART

Question: How can I truly know without any doubt that God is with me every moment? So often it seems that I am alone and on my own.

God is with you every second. If not, you wouldn't even be living. This is the proof: in order to live, you have to breathe. Are you breathing consciously every minute? Who is making you breathe? The One who wants you to live. And that's what you call God. Yes. Breathing itself is not in your hands. If you forget to breathe, God will make you breathe. Even if you don't want to breathe, God will force you to breathe. Can you exhale and stop breathing? No. The air is forced back into the body. Who does that? Somebody is interested in your living. God is in you, working through your body and mind every minute. There's no doubt about it. Believe in that, and allow God's hand to work through you. Your life will be better, easier and more happy. You are never alone. God is nearer to you than your own heart.

13 August

YOU ARE GIVEN A SCRIPT

Question: You say we are all actors. If we see someone in trouble, should we just say, "That is some act!" or even worse, "That's his karma?" Where do compassion and responsibility come in? Where does action come in?

Sri Gurudev: If you feel that you are an actor, it cannot just be theoretical. You have to experience it. If you have that sincere feeling, then you are totally in the hands of God. God will tell you what to do with that "star," whether to go and help him or ignore him. It's not even your business then. You cannot say, "I have to be compassionate," or "I have to ignore him. I have to decide that it's his karma." You are not deciding. Maybe that is his karma. God may not even present him to you. You may not even see him. If you really feel that God is working through you, and that you are an actor, that means you are not doing anything for yourself. You have been given a script; neither the words nor the actions are yours. You are asked to do certain things and you are just doing them, with total obedience. So let God decide what to do. He will tell you how to react. Otherwise it's a little bit of God and a little bit of you.

It's not that easy to feel, "Oh, yes, I'm just an instrument in the hands of God." We know the theory of it, and it is the truth, no doubt. We do nothing, nothing at all. That is plain fact. None of us is doing anything by himself or herself. It's all being done by a Higher Will. It's because of God's energy, God's consciousness working through you, that you seem to be doing a lot of things. There is a beautiful saying in the Koran: "Without the Will of God you cannot even tie your shoelace."

MAN PROPOSES, GOD DISPOSES

Whenever you feel that *you* are making a decision, then it is yours, not God's. If it just comes about, and is not something that you particularly decide, then it is God's decision. If you decide to do something and fail at achieving it, then that failure is also God's decision. We don't achieve all that we decide to attempt. That's why we say, "Man proposes; God disposes." Sometimes people seem to be achieving what they want. Probably those things are in agreement with God, and that is why those people are achieving them. But still, if a person thinks that *he* did something and *he* achieved it, then he is putting his ego there. So the individual should decide, "Am I planning out of my own ego, or are things just happening?" If you just allow them to happen, or if you feel, "God gave me the idea to plan this," or if it gets fulfilled and you say, "It is His plan, He made use of me. Let Him be happy, let the glory go to Him," then you don't get very excited about it and you don't look for the glory for yourself. When you don't look for that, you don't get disappointed. You just feel happy by having been a nice instrument in the hands of the Lord. That way is safer, because if it doesn't happen as you planned, you don't get disappointed. You just feel, "Probably that was God's will."

GOD WILL ANSWER YOUR PRAYERS

God is everywhere. You can talk to anything or anybody, and God will present Himself through that. A small stone or piece of paper can answer you. A picture or a small light can answer you. If you are looking for God in those things, it is not just a piece of paper or a stone or a piece of metal that you will see. It is God. That is what you are looking for, and that is what you see. When you sincerely look for God, He *has* to be present there and do His part.

In this age, God is more kind and more merciful. He doesn't demand much austerity. Even a little giving is enough. In those days when everything was beautiful, God demanded more. In this age, He knows that there are a lot of things to distract you. If you are going to think of Him even a little in the midst of all the distractions, that is a tremendous thing for Him. He will love you more. God does not look for quantity;He wants quality. Even if a little bit of sincere prayer is offered once from a devoted heart, that prayer will be answered. If your prayer is not answered, don't blame God. Probably it did not come from a one hundred percent sincere heart. Be more sincere. Cry and weep. Probably you might feel ashamed or embarrassed if you do that in front of others. So shut your door. Then there is no one else there but you and God. You can be totally free from any shame. And God *will* answer your prayers. There is no doubt about it. Let us develop that kind of faith and trust in God. Surrender to Him, and receive all the guidance. He is ready to pour out His Grace and guidance if we are ready to receive it.

16 August

BUT IF YOU CAN DO SOMETHING

Question: I hate fighting and find it very upsetting. Even fighting among dogs. Is there any way I can overcome being disturbed by it?

Sri Gurudev: You might not like fighting, but don't hate it. Hating is worse than fighting. Dogs fight, and the next minute they're together hugging each other. But when you hate, you keep on hating. So if you don't want to see fighting, you should learn to stay away from hating. What can you do when dogs fight? That's their nature. We are not going to stop everything in nature. But if you can do something instead of hating the fighting, do it. Maybe the dogs are fighting over a piece of bread. Buy a number of pieces and throw them everywhere so that each dog will have one. Then probably they won't fight. But if you hate, you lose the capacity to do something to stop the fighting.

THE ESSENCE IS ALWAYS THERE

Anything that becomes rare becomes very dear to us. When things are in abundance, we do not even know their value. It is only when a species is labeled "endangered" that we try to protect it. Even the value of peace has been taught to us in this way. Nature allowed us to do everything to lose our inner and outer peace; now we are beginning to know the greatness of having peace.

In the normal worldly sense, a species may become extinct. There is a beautiful saying in the Bhagavad Gita: "What *is* will always be. What is *not*, never was and never will be." The essence is always there. You can never destroy the essence. Then what is it that is destroyed? The form that the essence takes. Only the name and form are destroyed.

Species keep changing. We cannot stop that. All of a sudden hundreds of whales die and get washed ashore. Can you stop that? It is all part of the nature. Peace is also a species on the verge of extinction. The whole world is now striving to save it. Let us do whatever we can to help others and to not consciously hurt anyone or anything. That means that no one should be afraid of you and you do not have to be afraid of anyone. This is an important quality of a yogi or spiritual seeker. Fearlessness is an important virtue. Develop that.

18 August

DON'T WORRY ABOUT THE FUTURE

What you sow you reap. Don't worry about the future and don't worry about the past. A great thinker said the past and the future are not even visible. But what is visible? The golden present. Think of the golden present, sow what is necessary, what is right. Sow good thoughts, sow good deeds, and I am sure you will reap good fruits. There is no question about it. What you do comes back to you. What you sow, you reap. So do the right thing in the present, and don't worry about the future. The people who worry about the future miss the present as well. You have something right now. You have it in the hand, something nice to eat; don't think, "What will happen if I am hungry tomorrow?" By the time you find that out, someone will have snatched it from you. Always remember the golden present. Never miss it. A happier life is not given to you by someone else. Not even God can give you a happier life. Remember that. Happiness is in you. If you take care not to lose it, it is always there.

19 August

THE SIMPLE AND PRACTICAL WAY TO FIND PEACE

Any time anyone complains of worry, anxiety, depression, fear, hatred, jealousy—whatever it is—let him sit back and analyze the cause. If he is really sincere, he will find out that he wanted something for himself. Selfish desire causes all the problems. Do things for the sake of others, not for yourself. That is the simple and practical way to find peace.

20 August

THE CONSCIENCE IS THE SAME IN EVERYONE

Question: Should I ask, "What is Thy will?" for every decision, every day? Is that self-help, or am I being too dependent?

Sri Gurudev: In the beginning, until we learn what His will is, we have to be dependent. Who is the One who wills, and who is the one who wants to know the will? Both are within you. Your own spirit, which is the image of God or the Cosmic Soul, acts according to the Cosmic Will. So if you are asking to know His will, you are asking your own conscience. In that case, your will is: Let Thy will be done, not my egoistic will. In other words, follow your conscience, not your ego. Ego is your will; the will of the conscience is His will. Egos differ from person to person; but the conscience is the same, in everybody, in everything. Because we see many consciences, but the sum total of them is what you call Superconsciousness.

21 August

THE MASTER'S PRESENCE

Question: How should a disciple approach the master in thought and during meditation?

Sri Gurudev: Think of the teachings and try to apply them in your life. Then the master is with you always. A teacher is not some person; the *teaching* is the real teacher. If you follow the teaching, you will always have the teacher with you. Don't try to get the teacher into your heart; instead get the teaching into your heart. Keep it there, and you will feel your master's presence and guidance always.

THE WHOLE WORLD IS AN ALTAR

Question: What did Jesus mean when he said, "Take, eat; this is my body which was given for you."

Sri Gurudev: When he says, "It's my body," that means the bread itself is the manifestation of that spirit. Whatever you eat, eat it with the feeling that, "It is the spirit that has manifested as this food, and I am eating it." "My *body*" means the body of the spirit. It is the spirit expressing as the bread. So when you eat the bread you don't eat something ordinary, you eat the very spirit itself. Everything is God. God comes in the form of bread and you are eating it. So be thankful to God who has come in the form of bread. And if that feeling is there, you don't even have to go to the church to have Communion. Even when you go and buy a piece of bread in the market, it becomes Communion if you eat it with that feeling.

The whole world is the altar of God. Even when you eat something, it is the God in you that is eating. You are offering it to God. If we can only change our vision and the thought, whatever we do becomes spiritual practice. So, let our lives be a constant, constant service to God at the huge altar here. The whole world is an altar. Everything is God's manifestation. Whatever you do to somebody, you are doing to God. Not only to people—to animals, to plants, to everything.

23 August

IT'S AVAILABLE TO EVERYONE

Contentment is God. A contented mind is a peaceful mind; it is not disturbed. That is why we say, "Contentment is golden." If you are contented, your mind is always peaceful, serene. Then you are a yogi automatically. That's the only qualification. The sign of a good yogi is to be always peaceful, always contented. Once you experience that, you will not be running after things. The minute you stop running after things what happens? Things run after you.

If you can see that kind of quality in others, you will never feel jealousy. Instead, you will say, "Why don't I develop that?" God's blessings and grace are not given only to a select few. They are available to everyone.

LET US PLAY OUR ROLES WELL

Peace, contentment, not running after anything is what you call the kingdom of God. Once you achieve that kingdom of God, what will happen? Everything else will be running after you. Know that by knowing which everything else is known. Instead of running after things, let things run after you. Just be contented in your own peace and joy. Remain in the world, but offer your service to others, as the peace within you, the God within you, would prompt you. If He places you in a situation, fulfill that job. If He has hired you to be a wife, be a wife. Who knows, in the next birth He might hire you as a husband. Whatever role you are given, whatever makeup you put on, act your part very well.

We are all playing different parts in the drama. I have been given the part of a swami; you all have put on different makeup to sit there and listen to the swami. It's a drama. Tonight's performance. When the curtain falls, there's no swami and no audience. Ultimately all the chess pieces go into the same box. Before, there was no difference. After, there is no difference. In between, all these differences come because you have to play different parts. So let us play our roles well for the sake of the common good. Not for any selfish reason. That will help us to experience supreme peace at all times.

A SMALL BOWL OF WATER AND A NEEDLE

The person who wrote the great South Indian scripture, the Thirukkural, is Thiruvalluvar. He had a wife named Vaasuki. Every day when he sat to eat, along with a plate and glass, his wife placed a small bowl of water and a needle on the table. And every day when he finished the food, he would not have touched the needle or the bowl of water. Still, she used to put them there simply because he had asked her to. She never questioned it, because she respected him and knew he must have some good reason. She simply thought, "He asked me to do that and I am doing it. That's all."

But the time came, after many years of married life, that Vaasuki was lying on her deathbed. Thiruvalluvar, seeing his wife's sad face, questioned her, "Vaasuki, after all these years living with me and knowing the philosophy of life and death, why do you look like this? Are you afraid of dying?"

She replied, "No. Having lived with you, I understand what death means. I am not afraid of dying, but still I have an unanswered question in my mind. You know, every day when you ate I put a bowl of water and a needle on the table. I never saw you use them. I'm just wondering what they were for."

"Suppose I had spilled a grain of food," he explained. "I could have just pricked it with the needle, washed it in the water, and put it back on the plate to eat." If even one piece of rice had fallen, he would have taken it, washed it, and eaten it. That shows how respectful he was of food.

There are two things to be noted here. Vaasuki had never during their whole married life questioned her husband's request; and in all his life he had never spilled even one grain of rice.

26 August

WHO HAS BEEN FEEDING YOU ALL THESE DAYS?

One of my very first teachers was Sadhu Swamigal of Palani in South India. I spent several years with him in the very beginning of my spiritual life. He was a great *siddha* (spiritually accomplished one), and he was a great *tantric* yogi. Pure *tantric* yoga means doing *upasana* of the deities. *Upasana* means sitting next to God. When you use yantras and mantras you are using *tantra*. It's a sort of internal worship with total devotion. He was a great person and he had that kind of close communication with God. Very often at night we would hear him quietly talking to God, almost like a friend. His main deities were Lord Muruga and the bountiful Goddess, Mother Annapoorna. He did *upasana* of Annapoorna because he wanted to feed everyone. Even today, long after he left his body, his ashram still feeds thousands of people every day at Palani Hill. All the spiritual seekers and pilgrims around just go there and eat. We never knew where the provisions were going to come from, but they always came. Often rich people would come and give money to the ashram and say, "I want to feed two thousand people today in memory of my father," or something like that. Of course the ashram had huge vessels and the people who contributed the money would themselves come and serve.

But one day as we were about to retire, the person in charge of the provisions came and told myself and another swami, "The food's all gone. We cannot even make gruel for tomorrow. There's not even a single grain of rice. We don't know what to do."

Swamiji was sitting there on the veranda talking to some people. We went there, wringing our hands. "What is the matter?" he asked. "Swamiji, there is a crisis." "Hah! What is the crisis?" "There's not even a single grain of rice for tomorrow." He laughed and laughed, "Oh, I see. Terrific. What are you going to do?" "We don't know." "I see. Well, who has been feeding you all these days?" "Muruga. Annapoorna." "If you deserve it, you will be fed again tomorrow. Don't worry. Go to sleep." That's all he said, "If you deserve it, you will get your food. Go." And we simply had to go and retire.

At 12 o'clock midnight, a farmer from the next village came and knocked at the door. When we opened it, we saw two cartloads of rice bags. The farmer said, "I was just falling asleep when I had a dream. A beautiful lady dressed all in white appeared to me and said, 'Get up and take some rice to Sadhu Swamigal's ashram. Go right away. They need rice for tomorrow.' I didn't have the courage to question her. I simply put the rice in the carts and brought it here at once."

Imagine how we felt. Many times it happened, many times. We should have that kind of total trust in God. We should know that if God is going to provide for us, He will provide. We don't have to worry about it.

THERE'S NO NEED TO BE AFRAID

Put your faith in God. Then do whatever you can within your capacity, because you cannot do anything beyond your capacity. If you could do something beyond your capacity, then you would have the capacity to do it. So try your utmost, but at the same time, have faith in God: "God, I am doing all I can. But I still need Your help. I need Your strength. I don't have that much strength of my own." So, have that faith, and do it with sincere prayer. It is better to try than to be afraid. If, out of fear, you don't try it, how do you know whether you can do it or not? Sometimes when you try, you may do it and find your fear was just a waste. So there's no need to be afraid. Fear is not going to help us. Simply do it boldly, and God will help you. Remember God helps those who help themselves. If you have that kind of faith, there's no need to be afraid. Fear and faith don't go together. You say you have faith in God; God has all the strength, all the capacity, He's omnipresent, omnipotent. If you have that deep faith in a powerful God and if at the same time you say, "Oh, I am afraid of this, afraid of that," then you don't really believe in God. If you believe in God, you will think, "God will take care of me. I'm doing what I can." Even if something happens so that you don't get what you want, you don't need to be afraid. Your faith will say, "Well, maybe God didn't want me to have that." You accept it. "I wanted it. Yes. And I tried hard, but I didn't get it. Why? Because God didn't want me to have it. So I accept it."

If you have faith, you can move mountains. The problem is you cannot develop that kind of faith unless the mind is clean. You need a steady and pure mind, an undisturbed mind, that's not distracted by all kinds of worldly desires. A mind that's not contaminated by, "I, me, mine." Only in a pure mind can you develop that faith. If you have that faith you can achieve everything. Blessed are the pure in heart, they shall see God. That's the duty of every sincere seeker after truth—truth being permanent peace, permanent joy; experiencing God in the form of peace and joy within. There's no shortcut.

28 August

A HEART FREE FROM ATTACHMENT

Question: Please explain the meaning of Jesus' teaching, "It is easier for a camel to go through the eye of a needle than for a rich man to enter the kingdom of God."

Sri Gurudev: Poverty is not in things. You need food, shelter, a body. Poverty means giving up "mineness," or calling things "mine, mine, mine." A rich man, in this sense, is the one who thinks that he owns everything and possesses everything. A heart free from attachment is a poor heart. And it is only into such a heart that God can enter.

29 August

ALL THE REST IS JUST A DREAM

In the end, nobody—none of these so-called loved ones—is going to come with you. I don't say that you should deny them or renounce them. It's all right to be with them; but you have to save your soul. Nobody else is going to help you with that. How many individuals have left the world with the people they loved so much, or the money they loved so much, or the name they loved so much? None. Everything is soon forgotten. History tells us that. The only people the world remembers are the few who have really given themselves to God.

Put God first. That is the first and foremost thing to achieve. God is the only reality. All the rest is a dream.

30 August

SOW THE RIGHT SEED NOW

Question: Would you please speak about what you foresee in the future for the next ten or twenty years?

Sri Gurudev: I don't worry about the future. If you take care of the present, the future will be taken care of. What you sow now, you will reap. Don't just imagine, "After ten years I'll be having all kinds of fruits and flowers in my garden, and when they grow I will go and pick them and give them to everybody." Don't sit there and visualize it, and enjoy thinking that way and waste your time. Instead, take your time to go and dig a hole and put in at least one seed. Sow the right seed now. In the golden present. In a way, you are all sowing good seeds, yogic seeds. With people like you all over the world, there will be a wonderful future. This world will be a heaven very soon, no doubt. That's what I see. Many people say, "Oh, the world is going to collapse!" No. I have confidence that it is going to be a heaven. It's going to be filled with better people, people who love each other, care for each other. It's already happening, and you are the seeds for that.

LIVE ONLY TO SERVE

It is not possible for others to take advantage of one who serves selflessly. It could *appear* that way at times. But even if others seem to be taking advantage of you, that is to your advantage, because you are acting with a pure heart. You are doing whatever you can do to serve selflessly. Leave the rest to God, and do not worry about what others may think or interpret. The mere satisfaction of having done what you can do is enough. Otherwise you are looking for the results of your actions; that transforms them into selfish actions. Simply do whatever you can within your capacity. Remember: The dedicated ever enjoy Supreme Peace. Therefore, live only to serve.

September

1 September

GURUDEV'S PRAYER

Question: Could you suggest a prayer that would strengthen one's spirit when facing the difficulties of daily living?

Sri Gurudev: Would you like to know my prayer? My prayer is very simple. "Lord, I know that it is all Your form. It's all Your name. It's all Your deed. And it's all for good."

You are an instrument in the hands of the Super Consciousness; it functions through you as an individual consciousness. You are a little cell, and that Cosmic Consciousness makes you function. You don't do anything, so why worry about anything? All you have to do is know, "Yes, God is working through me. Credit or demerit goes to Him. I am not responsible. I am simply an instrument. God, I know you are the one who is using me."

If your life is like that, if you fully realize this truth, where is the difficulty for you? You are not even giving yourself into the hands of God. Who are you to even give? Simply know that you are already in the hands of God. Would you have any burden in life after such a realization? No. How peaceful you would be, how happy you would be.

So that's my prayer, "God, let me always remember that it is You and You alone working through this instrument. Whatever comes should go to You. It's not mine. People may praise me. Fine, the praise is Yours. By putting a garland around my neck, they are really honoring You. They may kick me out; it's You they are kicking. You are the one doing the kicking too. Having created me, You get the kick out of it. Why should I worry about it?"

I tell you, that's the simplest way. You can be totally, totally free from any problem in life. I'm positive about that.

BURDENS ARE SIMPLY ROCKS IN THE MIND

When you know why you are living and why you are working, that will give you strength. If you enjoy living, you enjoy working; the joy itself is enough to put a lot of strength in you. If you don't enjoy living and working, life becomes a burden to you and weakens you. People who don't enjoy their activities get tired very soon. If you really enjoy what you are doing, you will never get tired. Feeling tired is mainly in the mind. When you don't like something, it becomes very heavy to you. You carry it as a burden.

Suppose you are asked to carry a big rock. You might say, "Ohh, it's too much, I can't carry it." But suppose I give you a big bundle of gold coins even heavier than that rock? Somehow you will find the strength to drag it. That shows that burdens are simply rocks in the mind.

3 September

AND YOU STILL HAVE THE DIRTY SPOT

When others criticize you, there are two things to think of. First, "That's the way they look at me and that's what they see." Give them that freedom. Probably they may not see the other, better side. Feel sorry for them. Leave it at that.

The other thing to think about is, "Yes, he is like a mirror. Through him I see my defects." You go in front of a mirror to clean the dirty spots from your face. In the same way, this person is revealing your dirty spots. Thank the person and work on it. Then you will even look for criticism, because you can get help from that. If people don't criticize you, you will never know your own defects. If you see it in this light, you will never be angered by that. But if the mirror continues to show your dirty spot and you become defensive and punch it, you lose your mirror, you lose your fist and you still have the dirty spot.

4 September

SELF-HEALING SHOULD BE THAT WAY

By putting out positive thoughts, and correcting your mistakes, you can heal your problems. But don't do something to alleviate the problem without correcting the cause. The suffering came for your benefit. You should not try to take that away. Instead, bring out the nice things, the good qualities in you, the positive side in you, and the negative will get cured by itself. Self-healing should be that way. If you have some problem, ask yourself, "How did I get into this? What is the cause?" Then make a resolution: "Yes, in the future I will not encourage such thoughts. I will cultivate the opposite." The best way to drive away the darkness is to bring light into the room.

5 September

THERE IS NOTHING TO BE AFRAID OF

Sometimes we somehow get frightened, and a fear gets into the subconscious mind. Consciously din into the mind that you are immortal and that there is nothing to be afraid of. Think in a positive way. Boldly meditate on it. Convince your conscious mind, and let the conviction sink into the subconscious mind. You can even make a tape of your own, put it under your pillow, and literally sleep on it. It will slowly sink into your subconscious mind. The fear has gone into the subconscious, and you need to replace it with positive thoughts. So until the new ideas sink in, keep listening to them. Your mind is not completely sleeping, and your subconscious mind will still be listening to the tapes. When you are awake, consciously think of it, write down a reminder that you can read now and then. Put reminders everywhere until it's completely rooted out. Do all the positive things you can think of.

There are other ways also. But the yogic way is to put a new, opposite thought into the mind so that the undesirable thought will be squeezed out. And if you can't do it all by yourself, get help from others.

6 September

YOU ARE THAT IMMORTAL SOUL

Unless we realize our own true nature, unless we become aware of our spiritual reality, our life's purpose is not fulfilled. The main goal behind all these searches and approaches and actions is to realize our true nature, to realize the Self, the God within, and thus to realize that everything is the expression of that same Spirit. Until and unless that happens in our life, we will have to be born again and again. We will have to die many times. That is the one and only goal behind our existence.

It doesn't matter what you do, your goal should be to come close to this understanding: "Essentially I am God's spirit, I am the pure Self. I am Existence-Knowledge-Bliss Absolute." Ascertain your true nature, your spiritual nature. You are only functioning through this body and mind. They are your vehicles. You are *not* the body. You are *not* the mind. But you *are* that immortal soul.

FEW ARE WILLING TO PAY THE GREAT PRICE

There are only a few people who really want to reach something high and are willing to pay the price for it. That great price is discipline in life.

How much discipline is needed to send a man to the moon? How much is necessary even to make an Olympic champion? The athletes are not allowed to smoke. They have dietary restrictions; they have a curfew. They have to practice regularly. And it's all for a small piece of gold.

How much discipline is necessary to climb an ordinary mountain? And how much more discipline is required to climb Mount Everest? Here we are trying to climb the highest mountain: Ever Rest. All the great sages and saints said, "Discipline is necessary. Discipline your life. Control your senses." They were not fools.

We need places where we can learn discipline in life. It is in harnessing our energies that we get more benefit. Take hydroelectric energy, for example. Where do you get it? How do you get it? A free-flowing river is harnessed by a dam. Then the water is channeled through a big pipe. It runs through a turbine. And when the electricity is generated, it is stepped down by smaller transformers until it reaches your home. It is all discipline. If even one wire were exposed in your house, it would give you a shock or start a fire.

When you have a pet, and if you say, "Sit," and it sits, you are so happy, so proud. How many owners of pets show off how disciplined their pets are? What do you see in the circus? All the lions, tigers, elephants, and horses are disciplined. So don't ever forget that any achievement in life is based on discipline.

8 September

HE IS SHEDDING HIS LIGHT EVEN TODAY

We are extremely fortunate to celebrate the holy birthday of a great and modern saint of the world, His Holiness Sri Swami Sivanandaji Maharaj, who is shedding his light, even today, as he was doing one hundred years ago from those holy mountains, the Himalayas, on the banks of the Ganges River. It is very fortunate to even live in an age in which there are such great souls.

The scriptures say "The greatest bliss, the highest joy, embodiment of wisdom absolute, non-dual, boundless like the sky, He is the goal of 'Thou art That.' One, eternal, pure, and still, witness of the whole universe, beyond mind's grasp, of gunas free, to that guru may my worship be."

That means, the one who has all these qualities personified, he is the true guru. To him I give my salutations. Sri Swami Sivanandaji Maharaj is an embodiment of all these qualities. I feel very fortunate in having had him as my teacher, and to have seen his example even while he was functioning in the physical frame. If you see any little bit of truth or knowledge in me, it is the spark that came from that great Light. Being a small spark myself, it is almost impossible for me to fathom or talk about him. But let us take this occasion to remember a little bit of the real qualifications of a teacher; and at the same time to realize how lucky we are to have this association and how careful we should be in not missing this opportunity to realize that Light within. Life is limited; death can come at any moment. So, make hay while the sun shines. God bless you.

WE ARE REALLY FORTUNATE

The scriptures say that it is very, very difficult to get a human birth. We see millions of various species of life, but to be born as a human being is very rare. It is still more difficult to have a sane mind in a sound body. We must understand that well. It's not just an accident that we are in this beautiful, human frame. Certainly we have done millions and millions of meritorious deeds to qualify ourselves for this. A human birth is the only birth in which we can get liberated from the ocean of *samsara* or the constant ups and downs of life. This is our chance. This is the earning and learning place. That is why a human birth is a rare, rare privilege given to us. But that is only one of the three greatest blessings.

Even though you may have these things,the scriptures say to have a thirst to know the truth is even more rare. We see millions of people with a sound body and sane mind who have a thirst to accumulate a little money, name, fame. Name comes and goes. Money comes and goes. Even beauty comes and goes. A few wrinkles make us look old. So what is permanent? Only those things that are permanent are truth. The quest for the permanent, for the truth, is very rare.

Even if you have a human birth and the thirst to know the truth, there is something that is still more rare. To have someone to tell you where the truth is. A spiritual guide. There are many teachers who can help you to earn a little money, who can help you to beautify yourself or to get a little knowledge, but the ultimate truth is to be shown only by someone who has experienced the truth with the help of another person who got the truth. This truth passes from person to person. Spiritual teachers are very rare; and if you are lucky enough to find one you should realize how fortunate you are. That's how I felt when I met my Master. We are really fortunate to have such guidance and to remember his teachings and his greatness, how he shed light to millions of people without even leaving the Himalayas.

10 September

WHAT IS GOD?

What is it that you are seeking as a spiritual seeker? Spirit. Then you should see everything in these terms: "Is it spirit or non-spirit? Is it God? Is it peaceful or peaceless? Is it permanent or changing?" Every minute you should discriminate, "Will this disturb my peace, or help me to retain it?" If anything comes to you, your first and foremost question should be, "Is this going to disturb my peace?" If so, then don't accept it. You don't avoid such things to *get* more peace. Nothing can *add* more peace. Things can either disturb your peace or just be there without disturbing your peace. That's all. Either this or that. If something is going to disturb your peace, you should question, "Why should this disturb my peace? It's not disturbing the other person's peace. Is there anything wrong with the thing or with me?" Then you realize, "Yes, the mistake is with me. The thing by itself is not going to disturb me."

You can have all the wealth in the world and still not get disturbed by anything. On the other hand, you can renounce everything except one tiny little item and lose your peace over that one thing.

11 September

REAL PEACE IS IN THE MIDST OF TURMOIL

Question: It seems that whenever things are very calm and tranquil, one can be sure that some big turmoil will be happening at any moment. Will life always be like this? In moments of tranquility, must we always keep one eye watching for the enemy to come over the hill?

Sri Gurudev: Yes, it is better to watch for it. Life is always like that. It is in that quietness that the enemy comes to test how peaceful you are. If darkness comes, look for the light that follows. When the day comes, watch for the night that follows. If you know that one will not be there without the other, then you won't get caught in either. Absence of turmoil is not real peace. Real peace is when you rise above the turmoil, and stay peaceful in the midst of it.

EITHER YOU KEEP THE BASKET IN THE BOAT OR ON YOUR SHOULDER

Once a man was sailing in a small boat with a few other people. All of a sudden the boatman said, "The boat seems to be overloaded. The water is coming up higher and higher and we are about to capsize. If we want to stay afloat, we have lighten the load in the boat." Immediately the man said, "Oh, don't worry; I can take care of it." He had a heavy basket in the bottom of the boat, so he picked it up and put it on his head. "Is it okay now?" It was a heavy basket, so he thought, "I will just carry the basket and reduce the weight in the boat."

Whenever you say, "I did it," you are carrying your basket while sitting in the boat. The truth is, no matter where the basket is, all of the weight is being carried by the boat. Whether you keep it in the bottom of the boat or on your head is immaterial. As long as you feel that *you* are carrying it, *you* are responsible, *you* are doing something, fine, then carry it. The Lord just smiles: "All right, let him carry it." But if you decide to put the weight on *His* shoulder, He is ready and willing to carry it. The freedom is there. You can either keep the basket in the boat, or on your head. Sensible people will keep it in the boat; egoistic people will keep it on their head, that's all. Ultimately, the whole weight is being carried by Him.

13 September

THAT'S WHY IT'S CALLED A DREAM

Don't worry too much about dreams. If you have a dream about someone else— about his or her health, or whatever it is—it's just a warning. It need not always come true. So you can just tell the person, "I feel that you should be a little more careful." There's nothing wrong in advising someone that way. Even if the dream is a false dream, he or she doesn't lose anything by being a little more careful. You are not hurting anyone. If the dream is about you and there is something that you can do to be more careful, do it. If the dream doesn't make any sense, just drop it. Not all dreams are absolute truth. Some are meaningless. The mind functions on various levels. So don't worry too much about it. You yourself will know clearly, "Yes, these are some of the dreams that I should pay attention to. I should be more careful." If you don't find any sense to some of the dreams, ignore them.

If God wants to speak to you through a dream, He will give some clarity also. God will not tell you something without enabling you to understand it. If you don't really understand, you could say: "God, I don't know why the dream came. If it is the one that You sent me, I don't seem to understand. Maybe tomorrow night you can clarify it." Otherwise just drop it. Anything that you don't clearly understand, just ignore; because a dream need not always be true. That's why it's called a dream.

14 September

IT'S SUPER SURRENDER

Question: Do we have to accept whatever karma comes, or can we try to change it a little bit?

Sri Gurudev: If we know that we are instruments, and nothing is in our hands, then accepting and changing are not in our hands either. It's very simple. If you are prompted to accept, then accept it. If you are prompted to change, then change it. Even that will be prompted. Something will tell you, "Come on, go ahead and try to change it." Then your answer should be, "Okay, God, if that's what You want, let me do it with Your backing. You are prompting me, so I am doing it." It's super surrender, and life is really beautiful that way. All you have to do is follow His lead. The brush never tells you, "Oh, touch here, touch there, use a broader stroke." You simply be the brush, and let Him paint whatever He wants. He is seeing the whole picture, and it will be a masterpiece.

WE ARE ALL WALKING TEMPLES

Worshipping God does not mean that God is in front of you and you worship Him directly. Serving people is worshipping God; doing things for people is doing things for God. The great saint Thirumular said, "If you worship in the stationary temple, it only reaches God there; it won't reach God in the walking temples. But if you worship God in the walking temples, it will also reach Him in the stationary one." We are all walking temples. Your body is your temple. The Lord is inside you. Your heart is His altar.

That means service to humanity is worship of God. If you worship God only in the church or synagogue, humanity is not going to be benefited. God does not need your service for Himself. He doesn't need a temple. There is God in everyone. If you give someone some food, you are offering it to the God residing in him or her. If you repair a vehicle, you are repairing it so that God can drive around. The real reward in doing things is seeing how many others will be benefited by them.

THE TEACHER DOESN'T LOOK FOR ANYTHING ELSE

Question: How does a master love his disciples? How did you as a disciple learn to love?

Sri Gurudev: "How does a master love his devotees?" You will certainly know it when you become the master. A true master loves not only his or her devotees, but loves everybody and everything equally. There are no gradations; his love for everybody is the same. Sometimes it might *appear* to be a little more for the disciples just because they are nearby and they are following the teachings. It might look as if he loves them more. Sometimes he might even say, "I love you more than anybody." Probably that is one way of encouraging you. It need not be true. Don't get carried away by that. Just to encourage and inspire you, he could say, "Oh, you are the most beloved devotee." It's for your benefit. But to him everyone is the same because his love is unconditional. Whether you follow the teachings or not, whether you praise him or blame him. You might go and backbite. You might even renounce him or denounce him. It doesn't matter; you are still the same to him. Pure love doesn't look for any return. And that is true love. Everyone should learn to love that way.

The question now is, "How did you as a disciple learn to love?" There again, I don't think I ever learned to love. It's not something that you learn. It's spontaneous. It just comes from the heart. Nobody needs to teach you. When you see something beautiful, something greater than you, and you feel that you are receiving a lot, what can you return? You cannot return all that you get from a teacher and probably the teacher doesn't need any return. He doesn't even expect your love. But from your side, you can return that just by loving. By loving that person, you love the teaching. You love everything that you get from the person. Because you love it, you cherish it and use it in your life. It's not that you just love the teaching and put it aside. You apply it in your very life. That's the only way you can express your genuine love to the teacher. The teacher doesn't look for anything else.

17 September

IT'S IMPOSSIBLE TO MAKE A WRONG DECISION

It is impossible to make a wrong decision. Even if you make a wrong decision, you will very soon know it is wrong and so you will learn a good lesson. It is worse not to make any decision at all. If you don't make any decision, you will not grow. If you want to do the right thing and you don't know what to do, there are many people who can help you. Ask some people in whom you have confidence, and follow their advice. Because ultimately, it's all for good. Even if you make a mistake, it's for good, because it teaches you that it's a mistake. You don't really lose anything.

THIS IS A COSMIC MISSION

If you simply put your trust completely in that great force, all your burdens will be lifted. You will be led to perform your mission. You should know that you have been sent here for a purpose. It's not that you decided one fine morning, "Let me go and take birth in America or on this planet." You did not decide that. Someone else has decided, "So-and-so should go, take birth in such-and-such a place with a certain identity." And there is a purpose for that. "I am sending this person to do this and this and this and this. Until that is over, I will keep him there. Once the job is over, I will fire him." In a way we are all hired by a higher authority. And we have to do our part. Once the job is over, you will be called in. God is a great economist also. He will not waste even an ounce of extra breath on you. Yes. It's all measured; He sent you packaged with a certain amount of breath.

So it's not *our* job. This is a cosmic mission. We are all doing our part. Let us do it consciously. "It's all God's work. God has sent me to do something. God has given me all the necessary things to fulfill my job, to perform my duty; and He is behind me making me do things also. I don't have to worry about anything." We unnecessarily take many a responsibility upon our shoulders: "I have to do this. I'm responsible for it." No. None of us is responsible for anything. If we have any responsibility, it is to know the Truth. Let us know the Truth. "My responsibility is to know who sent me and for what purpose, and to allow that unseen hand to function through me." Don't put up impediments. He's going to make you do it anyway, so why not just do it comfortably instead of saying, "No, I can't, I can't."

19 September

REAL FREEDOM

Happiness never comes from outside. Only when you are not depending on anything from outside for your happiness are you totally independent. You may live in a free country, but you are not free until and unless you free yourself from ignorance. National freedom is not the real freedom. You are not even free to change lanes as you want. If you don't give the proper signal before you change lanes, you will hear the police siren coming behind you. Can you say that you are really free? Real freedom comes only when you know your true nature.

THINK WELL AND YOU WILL BE WELL

Just do what you can, and leave the rest to Nature. Nature constantly says, "Be that so." We say, "Ahh, I want to be a monkey." Be that so. "I want to be an intelligent man." Be that so. "I am very unhappy." Be that so. "I am sick of the whole thing." Be that so. Whatever you think, Nature says, "Let it be so."

So it's up to you. If you keep on thinking negative things, Nature will say, "Be that so. Let it be so." Because you wanted it, you got it. So you see how careful we should be even in our thoughts.Whatever you think is blessed by the cosmic force. "Be it so." That's why we say, "As you think, so you become." Think well; you will be well. Think ill; you will be ill. It's all your thought. Sometimes you don't think ill of yourself, but you think of others' ills. What will happen? When you think of that, you will become that. We say, "See no evil, hear no evil, speak no evil." Why? Because if you see evil, hear evil or speak evil, you will become evil. You may think, "So-and-so is an evil fellow; so where is the harm in my saying that?" Yes, he may be an evil fellow all right, but what are you thinking of? His evil qualities. When you keep thinking of evil qualities, that is what you become. You are not hurting him, but you are hurting yourself. That's why we should always think well, think well, think well in our lives. Always see good things. Train your eyes to see the bright side of everything.

LINK YOURSELF WITH AN UNLIMITED CAPACITY

Your destiny is your own creation. It is because you are the master of your destiny, and *you* did it, that you can always undo it. When you have the capacity to do something, don't you have the capacity to undo it? So trust in that capacity, and then go forward.

Sincerity in seeking comes only when you know that you have a limited capacity. Then you link yourself with an unlimited capacity. Asking for help also is like that. Only when you say, "I can't do it anymore, please help me," does the help come.

Sometimes God seems to be a hard-hearted person. He waits until you really, really give up. Until then, your prayers are not really sincere. They may be beautiful. You may sing nice songs. You may have a good voice. Your chants may be wonderful, your Indian chants or Gregorian chants. But when you cry, you don't worry about your voice, about the tune, about a pitch. It's simply, "Ohhh, my God, please!" You shout it. Yes. And that is what you call sincere prayer. It should come from the very heart, not from the head. That prayer is heard immediately. So let us become that kind of seeker. Let's be sincere and serious. We should be totally convinced that, "I am nothing. My capacities are very limited. Without that unlimited source I can't do much." It is that energy that makes this body sit here today, and that body sit there. We are all being used by the same energy.

LITTLE BY LITTLE, THE PEACE WILL COME

Peace is not just in the hands of a few individuals. Every one of us can do something. When there are more peaceful individuals, the world becomes more peaceful. So let it begin within oneself. In one sense, it is almost impossible to make the whole world peaceful. The world is not created that way. It has differences, varieties, though the basis is the same, the spirit is the same. God created everything and everybody differently. We need all kinds of people to make the world drama go well. Even the terrible sinner has a place. We have no right to condemn anyone. But we can set good examples for others to follow.

The world is full of ups and downs, positive and negative. It's like a big factory. Human beings come in as raw material, and they are in the process of becoming perfect. Look at a Detroit car factory. At one end you see the beautiful finished cars, ready to be shipped out, but what do you see at the other end? All crude, raw materials. Metal sheets, nuts and bolts, that go through processing. A lot of cutting, chipping, rubbing, scrubbing, chiseling, filing, grinding, welding, pressing. Slowly, it takes shape. People are like that also. That's what you call evolution or growth. Through that we gain experience, we learn. Even a sinner is there to show you what is not to be done. He's an example for you. By seeing him, you realize, "Oh, I shouldn't do that."

So it's really not possible to find the world one hundred percent peaceful at any given moment. But people can individually find peace, and then set examples for others. Little by little, little by little, the peace will come.

LIFE IS ALSO A PILGRIMAGE

Question: When you went to Mount Kailash and reached the goal of the pilgrimage, the abode of Lord Siva, was there something to be experienced? What was it like?

Sri Gurudev: *Gurudev sighs and leans back in his chair with his eyes closed. For a moment he is lost in reverie, with a radiant expression on his face.* There is no way to describe that experience. It's almost like saying, yes, you worked hard, you accomplished a lot, came home, had a nice shower, went into the kitchen and had some supper, then came to your bedroom, turned on some soft music, had a warm drink, turned down the lights and then prepared the bed, lay down, covered yourself with a blanket, closed your eyes, repeated your mantram and then...

What would you say the next morning if someone asks you, "What did you experience? Tell me?" You cannot put into words what you experience. We can use our limited ability and say, "A great relief, a peace and ease. As if all your burdens have been taken away and you are simply floating." What you experience at the end of the pilgrimage is really very hard to explain, but the entire journey prepares you for it. Every minute you experience God's hand at work. Every minute. Several times I almost said goodbye; but by His grace, I came back again.

So, all of these things in a way prepare us by showing us that without His help we cannot do anything. Nothing that we own, nothing that we call ours will help us to experience God within and without. You might have a strong body; but when there is no oxygen, what are you going to do? You may have millions of dollars, but there is nothing to buy. So everything becomes nothing. In a way, you are made to learn the worthlessness of everything that you have depended upon. It is at that point that you say, "It's only God's grace that helps me."

Truly, God is everywhere. It's not that God can be seen only in that spot. But because you paid such a big price, you can more easily recognize Him there. So pilgrimages prepare you for that experience. You literally live with God. Life is also a pilgrimage, to prepare us for that experience of realizing that God is everywhere, within and without.

24 September

HOW MANY PEOPLE GO TO JERUSALEM FOR A PICNIC?

Everything can be a pilgrimage. Even going from this building to the next building can become a pilgrimage. Yes. It's all in your attitude. Unfortunately you only call it a pilgrimage when you travel to a holy place because that's the only time you feel that way. It's the feeling that makes it a pilgrimage. How many people go to Jerusalem for a picnic? Just because it's a holy city, that doesn't mean everyone who goes there is on a pilgrimage.

Pilgrimage is in the mind. If you could create the same attitude even while going around your own city, it would be a pilgrimage. If you go to New York and come back, it's a pilgrimage if you go with the right attitude. Where do you want to go for a pilgrimage? You don't need to go to Mount Kailash nowadays. If you just walk back and forth across the street in New York a few times you will face more obstacles and more danger. Just walk along Broadway; how many distractions are there, how many obstructions? So it is the attitude with which you go that makes the difference.

25 September

IT'S NEVER TOO LATE

Question: During my life I have spent most of my time in ignorance and selfishness. Only now do I realize that the most important thing is to seek God only. Could I hope that one day the inner joy will also happen inside me, or is it too late in this life?

Sri Gurudev: It sounds as if you are 99 years old! It's never too late to realize the Truth. Our age is not limited to the age of the body. Remember that. You will never be spared until you realize. It's a sort of compulsory education. You cannot quit school and get out of it. Wherever you go, there will be a classroom. There will be a teacher waiting to teach you. You have to learn it today or tomorrow or next year or in the next life or after ten lives. That means after ten bodies. Until we learn the Truth, we will be given body after body after body. So how can you say it's too late? It's never too late. At the same time, know that it doesn't really take that much time to save yourself, or to know God, or to know the Truth. If your life is filled with dedication and renunciation, there's nothing to color or cover your vision. And when your vision becomes clear, you immediately experience the Truth.

26 September

GOD PROBABLY PURPOSELY CREATED A BOY LIKE THAT

Question: I understand that we are not to hate Hitler. But are we to love him?

Sri Gurudev: Certainly. He is also a child of God. The same God whom you love created him too. He was a naughty brother, that's all. He was also your own brother. He came into the same family. If your own brother became violent, what would you do? Would you hate him? You would love him, but you would correct him. You would stop him from doing the wrong things, but you would not hate him.

By hating such people what do you gain? You are hating yourself then. Hating is not the answer. It doesn't take you anywhere. If you still want to hate someone, hate the one who created you and him. Yes. That's what I tell those people who really want to hate Hitler. It's your own God whom you love, who you say is all merciful, that created him. Why should that God create such a fellow? It's the mistake of God then. Hate Him. Destroy all His places. Don't build any temples for Him, synagogues for Him. But if you love your God, then accept that God probably created a boy like that purposely, probably to teach us a lesson. By hating, we don't accomplish anything.

27 September

EVEN ONCE

We can all pray, "Thy Will be done. It's all Your Grace. It's all for good." We believe it; but when it comes to putting that belief into practice, we might fail because the mind is not yet clean. A prayer is heard if it is uttered even once with a clean mind. Even once. You don't need to repeat the prayer hundreds of times. No. God is not deaf; there is no need to repeat it again and again and again. You don't even need to say it out loud. He knows even your thoughts. But He also knows we are all hypocrites. We don't really mean what we say. We often pray just for show. God knows all that. So if we say it even once with complete sincerity—just once—that's all He needs.

28 September

SELF-HEALING IS POSSIBLE

We should know that the breath—the *prana*, or life force—and the mind are intertwined. Wherever one goes, the other follows. When the mind becomes agitated, the breath becomes agitated. When the mind is totally peaceful, the breath almost comes to a stop. So in the same way you can direct the *prana* with your thoughts. For example, if you look at your thumb and think, "I am going to make the thumb warm," think "warm," and not "hot," or you might get a blister. Yes. If your thinking is very concentrated and you are totally one-pointed as you send your thoughts to the thumb, all of the *prana* and blood will rush there, and you will get heat. In that way, you can send the vital energy wherever you want.

The same principle applies to healing also. By sending your thoughts to any affected part, you send your *prana*. Self-healing is possible. In a way, even when you pray for healing that's what you are doing. You trust that the higher power, God, is helping you to heal that. And you believe it, is it not so? So you are communicating with the higher power, and that energy automatically goes to the affected part along with your little energy.

29 September

REAL COURAGE

Only a very few are born with courage. Most people are weak; it takes a long time for them to build up courage. It takes real courage to understand the truth. Real courage means to give up "I, me, mine." It's not courageous to gather things. What we normally call courage is getting Gold Medals, Bronze Medals, fighting, winning, gaining. A "courageous" person jumps from a plane with a parachute three thousand feet up in the air. But the real courage is to give up everything and say, "I own nothing." Very few are courageous enough to renounce everything in the name of God, in the name of service to humanity.

You might call somebody courageous who comes and gives a nice punch to a person and all the person's teeth fall out. But if the fellow who got the hit smiles at him, "Is that all you are capable of? It doesn't matter, don't worry. Maybe you haven't learned the lesson yet. I forgive you," who is courageous then? The one who hit, or the one who smiled and lovingly forgave him? It takes more courage to forgive someone. And much more courage to forget. Even after forgiving, you might still remember. But to forget takes a lot of courage, a lot of training of the mind.

30 September

WHAT IS IT THAT YOU HAVE GAINED?

Bondage and liberation are within you. You bind yourself and you have to liberate yourself. If you don't want to part with something and depend on that for your happiness, then you are not independent. What is independence? Not to depend on anything, at any time.

A few centuries ago a chief minister of a country suddenly got into a spirit of renunciation and said, "I don't want to possess anything anymore. I just want to be free." So he renounced his job and his house and said, "The sky is my roof, the whole world is my house and God is my Father." Then he went and sat in front of a temple. He had been a very nice, capable chief minister. When he suddenly left everything, the king became upset and sent a messenger asking the minister to come back. But the minister said, "No, I am no longer interested in that job." Then the king decided to go see the minister himself. He found where the minister was sitting and stood in front of him, "Swami?" "Yes?" "Do you recognize me?" "Yes, I recognize you." "Please tell me what it is that you have gained by leaving everything to sit here like this." The minister looked at the king and said, "Until yesterday I was standing and you were sitting. Today I am sitting and you are standing. That is the first gain."

That is the greatness of renouncing your selfish life. You will not be afraid of anyone. If you're honest, you will be fearless. And when you're fearless, you're powerful. Ego will never make you powerful. You may appear to be powerful, but you are not truly powerful. The most egoistic people are the most fearful people, because they are constantly afraid of getting their ego hurt. They want to get everything they want, and if something is denied, immediately they get hurt. But a selfless person who is honest and has a clear mind, who is a righteous person, is always powerful. He doesn't need to worry about anybody.

October

1 October

LET THAT BE YOUR NATURE: LOVING AND GIVING

Once a man went to a river for a bath and found that the river was in flood. As he approached the rushing water, he saw a scorpion being carried away by the current. He took pity on it and thought, "Ohh, he is going to die." So he reached forward and took the scorpion out of the water. As he was taking it out, the scorpion stung his hand. As he got stung, he jumped and the scorpion fell back into the water. Again he felt pity, "Oh, I am so sorry. No, I will not let you die." He took it out, got another sting and again dropped it.

A friend was standing behind him watching the whole thing. As he reached in to take the scorpion out of the water one more time, the friend said, "You fool. Every time you pick up the scorpion, it stings you. Don't you have any common sense?" "Well,'" the man said, "I don't know about common sense. All I know is my nature is to feel pity for something, to be compassionate and, if possible, to save it. That is just the way I am." The friend replied, "But don't you see that the scorpion is stinging you and will continue to sting you?" The man explained, "What can I do? That is its nature. I cannot change its nature. And in the same way, you cannot change my nature." He did not hate the scorpion because he understood and accepted the nature of the scorpion. Let our nature be like this. That is our true nature: loving and giving. Of course, you can probably use a stick to lift the scorpion out.

2 October

WALK ON THE EARTH LIKE LIBERATED GODS

Human birth is a great opportunity for us. According to the Hindu and Buddhist philosophies, which believe in reincarnation, you have been passing through hundreds and thousands of births. Now you have been given this human birth, where you have a little freedom to think, to find out the ways and means to get out of the continuous cycle. This is the opportunity. If you are going to miss this, you don't know when you will have another chance. You might get caught in the whirlpool again.

So don't waste this life. Human life is not just to satisfy the senses. We have done that before in many other births. Even an animal eats, sleeps, begets children. They marry, even without the help of a priest or rabbi. What are you doing beyond that? You may earn a lot of money and build skyscrapers; haven't you seen birds building beautiful hanging palaces? They swing in the air. Can you build a nest like that? Can you build an anthill? How many special separate apartments are there in the anthill? Who is the architect, who is the engineer? Where did they study? In your colleges and universities? We are so proud, but the animals just laugh at us. In what way are we superior then? Not by building houses and comfortable vehicles or begetting more children or making ourselves beautiful. You can never make yourself more beautiful than a peacock, however much you rub, scrub and put on makeup. A butterfly is a thousand times more beautiful than you and I.

What is it that we want then? The only thing that differentiates man from the other animals is the urge to get out of this vicious cycle, to know our true nature. That is our first and foremost duty. If we miss this opportunity, no one knows when we are going to get it again.

Get out of this whirlpool while there is still time and energy. Become great servants of humanity. Renounce all the selfish shells. Be liberated. Walk on the earth like liberated gods, representations of God, the true children of God. Shed the light of God wherever you go. Let people see the light in you and see their light with the help of your light.

3 October

WHAT CAME FOR YOUR HEAD TOOK AWAY YOUR HAT

Selfish thoughts disturb the mind. When the mind is disturbed, the body gets disturbed. This is how some accidents occur. That is why the condition of the mind is very important. If the mind is serene and peaceful, many accidents could be avoided.

By keeping your mind calm, you can win over your karma. If you change your mind you can annihilate your karma. It is not necessary for the karma to bind you. If you have peace of mind, even if karma comes you may not know it. It will just come. There is a South Indian saying, "What came for your head, took away your hat." The karma came to take your head, but because of your peace of mind and presence of mind, it just took your hat away. That was enough to nullify the karma.

Even if the karma is really going to affect you, let it affect you. But remain peaceful. Stay calm. Don't give room for thoughts such as, "Ohhh, karma is more powerful, somehow it is going to affect me terribly!" Then you are already affected. Even the very thought, "No, I think it will never leave me alone," invites the karma to come and then it *will* come. Just stay calm, cool and live in the golden present.

4 October

WE HAVE TO TAKE CARE OF BOTH

The mind's physical expression is what you call the body. It is the mind that makes the body. Change the mind, and you can change the body. That is why your face changes when your mind is happy. It glows. People do not see your mind, but they see your face. When your mind is unhappy, don't they say, "Hey, what's wrong?" Why? Because the face expresses the mind. Every cell will listen to the mind and get changed according to its moods. That is why when you are in a very depressed state, you cannot even get up or do anything. You say, "Ohh, I can't do a thing today. I'm so upset." Getting upset is in the mind. The body should be able to get up and jump and play games, but it cannot because the body and mind are interconnected. If one falls sick, the other will also fall sick. That is why we have to take care of both.

5 October

YOU ARE THE PURE SPIRIT

You are the pure spirit. The body was created; it is part of the nature. But do not identify yourself as the body. That becomes a good excuse for us sometimes. A good excuse to be a lazy fellow. Heaven and hell are within; they are your own creation. You create your own Satan, your own darkness. Do not get caught up in all these things. Always identify yourself as the pure spirit. "I am using the body, using the mind." "*Chidaanand Chidaanand Chidaananda Ham. Hara Halume Alamastu Sat Chid Aananda Ham.*" That means: "I am not the body, not the mind, Immortal Self I am!" Sing it loud! Especially when you feel that your mind is a little depressed and you have allowed yourself to be affected by that. Instead, get up and say, "I am *not* the body, *not* the mind, Immortal Self I am! In all conditions I am Knowledge-Bliss Absolute!" Shout! Shake off the darkness. Remember your True Nature!

6 October

OTHERWISE HOW CAN YOU PROVE YOURSELF?

Put yourself in the hands of the higher force. You cannot do everything by yourself. If you believe in God, if you trust God wholeheartedly, even your sickness will go away because you are putting yourself into the hands of a more powerful doctor. Difficult situations come to give us a chance to prove that we trust in a higher energy. Otherwise,how can you ever prove yourself? When everything goes smoothly you are all good devotees, no doubt. But you really prove it when everything is shaking and still you are able to say, "It doesn't matter. Even if I lose everything, I am not going to lose this faith." Once you prove that, then everything that was lost will come back to you. That needs tremendous faith. Without faith no one can become a spiritual seeker.

7 October

IT DIDN'T MATTER WHO SAID WHAT, IT ALL CAME FROM RAM

There was a great saint by the name of Swami Ramdas. Some of you might have heard of him. Ramdas was an example of total surrender to the Lord in the form of Ram. His name was fitting: Ramdas, the servant of Ram. He saw Ram in every face. Somebody once said to him, "Why don't you go to Benares?" "Ahh, Okay. Maybe Ram told me. All right. Well, how should I go?" "Go to the railway station and take the train." He went to the railway station, and when the train came, he got on. The ticket collector said, "Where is your ticket?" "Oh, Ram didn't tell me about that." "Well, you can't continue." "Okay, what do you want me to do?" "You have to get off at the next station." "Fine." He got off at the next station, "Because Ram asked me to get out, I got out; that's all." So he just sat there on the platform until somebody came and said, "Why are you sitting here?" "Ram wanted me to sit here." "How did you come here?" "Oh, Ram said I should go to Benares on the train, and again Ram came and asked me to get off." "Oh, that's not right. You are simply listening to every Tom, Dick and Harry." "No, it's Ram. Ram as Dick. Ram as Harry. The same Ram." "So who am I?" "You are also Ram." "Okay, all right, stand up." "Okay." "Sit down." He sat. "Stand up." That fellow made him stand up and sit down fifteen times. Still, he felt, "Ram said so; all right, I'll do it." Finally the fellow realized the greatness of this person; he felt terrible and fell at Ramdas' feet saying, "I'm so sorry." "Oh, Ram, you shouldn't do that." "Come on, come on, the next train is bound for Benares, you get on." "All right." It didn't matter who said what; to him it all came from Ram.

8 October

IT ALL BOILS DOWN TO THIS ONE THING

A great saint by the name of Manickavasagar said, "Lord, You know what I want. And You will give me everything that I need. If by any chance, with my own little egoistic self, I feel that I want something, I should know that even that want is created by You. Without You, I wouldn't even have a want. If it is *my* want, it will never get fulfilled. So I leave it to You. You give me whatever You need for Your service. The minute You think that I have finished with that tool and I don't need it anymore, take it away."

It all boils down to this one thing: faith in a higher power. An unseen hand that constantly molds. "You put me here, I am here. You gave me this job, I am doing it." There's no superiority, inferiority. No "How come he is doing that, while I am doing this?" No. God selects each one for His work, and He gives various jobs to various people. Everything is equally great. There is nothing superior or inferior. Do every job joyfully as God's work. In the process of working, if your mind goes through some turmoil, suspicion or doubt, it will get cleared up when you meditate. All the problems that you created in your doing are undone by meditating. That's why meditation is so important.

9 October

IF YOU HAVE COMPLETE FAITH, ONE MANTRAM IS ENOUGH FOR EVERYTHING

Through sound you can create anything. There is no limit. The whole universe was created with sound. That is the power of the mantram. But unfortunately many who have a mantram do not even seem to realize its power. If you do not have faith in it, even though it is powerful, you will not experience it. When you do not have faith, naturally you will not repeat it much. Whether you have faith in it or not, if you put your finger in the fire it will burn. But you have to put your finger in the fire to get the experience. Whether you believe in the mantram or not, repeat it. Then you will know what it can do. The smaller the mantram, the bigger the power. Anything that is atomized gets more power. The more powerful mantrams will take a little longer time to bring the benefit. But of course your faith will enhance it; it gets a little more charged with a little love. The other way is very dry, but still, if you keep repeating it the faith will come. It will come whether you want it to or not.

You do not need to have a lot of mantrams for different purposes. No. Sometimes, when you say, "Oh, he is starting a journey, let us repeat a special mantram for his safety," I laugh at it, but I say, "All right, let them do it." Why a special mantram all of a sudden? What happened to your own mantram? Can't your personal mantram take care of that journey? It will take care of everything. The personal mantram is enough; but sometimes our faith in our own mantram is limited. We think that unless we repeat something especially for that purpose, it won't be useful. So for that sake, all right, go ahead, do it. But if you have complete faith, one mantram is enough for everything. It will take care of all of your trips, your problems, your diseases—or even someone else's. That is why you do not need to have so many things; just have faith, faith, faith.

FOR THE ONE WHO WEAVES, THERE'S NO NEED FOR A MONKEY

Learn the lesson, "God, You sent me here for a purpose. You know what to give me, how much to give me, when to give it to me, and how to give it to me, in order for me to do my part of the work. If I need some instrument, You will give me that. If I need some companion, You will give me that companion. If I need some money to do my service to You, You will send me the money." The mere fact that you are not getting something means that God thinks you don't need it. How nice life would be if we could just remember this. If you don't get it, think, "God probably thinks I don't need it. If I need it, even if I say, 'No, I don't want it,' He will force it into my hand."

There is a beautiful South Indian proverb, "For the one who weaves, there's no need for a monkey." When you use a hand-weaving machine, you work with delicate, thin yarns. And if you have a monkey for a pet, you are not going to weave much of anything. Because, as you know, monkeys like to imitate everything. So that means if you are interested in weaving, you shouldn't keep a monkey as a pet.

If God created you for weaving, He won't give you a monkey even if you want it. If He decides to give you a monkey, He will train the monkey to help you in weaving. Maybe to push the shuttle. We should have that kind of faith. That kind of acceptance won't come unless you have tremendous faith in God. Tremendous faith in a higher force, in the consciousness that sent you here, and that functions through you.

LEARN TO LOVE EVERYONE EQUALLY

What is the sign of a wise person, a godly person? He or she loves everyone equally, unconditionally, no matter what. Even the fellow who denies God is loved by God, is it not so? If God did not love the fellow who denies Him, He would immediately take the life force away from him. Why would He even keep him alive? If God does not want His scriptures to be burned, He will keep all the matchboxes away from that fellow. It's not impossible for God. God loves not only the person who praises Him, who builds churches for Him, who talks nicely about Him, but even the one who denies Him. That is what you call Cosmic Love.

You do not need to be doing great things. In your own small way, among your neighbors, around your house, see that you are a friend to everyone. Learn to love everyone equally, no matter what he or she is.

12 October

IT'S POSSIBLE THIS MOMENT

Question: Is liberation possible for me in this lifetime?

Sri Gurudev: Sure, it is. It is possible right now. Just don't bind yourself. You are already liberated, right at this moment. Why do you say in this lifetime? This *moment* you are liberated. Just see that you don't bind yourself.

13 October

YOU ARE MARRIED TO GOD ALREADY

Question: What is the best way to handle being attracted to or distracted by someone?

Sri Gurudev: If you are attracted to someone, deal with it by saying, "You are very attractive. Thank you. God has created you as an attractive person, wonderful. Keep yourself attractive." Bless the person. If you get distracted by that person, stay away a little. Because the distraction to your mind is worse than getting him or her. What is the use of getting the person and losing your peace? Peace is more important. There is a pretty young man or young woman always with you: the peace within. You are wedded to that. God has given you that. We are all married to that peace. Let us not disturb it or divorce it to get someone else. If others come without disturbing your peace, wonderful. But if anything is going to disturb your peace and separate you from your first wed partner, say, "I am already married, thank you." That peace is what you call God. You are married already to God. He is the only husband. We are all wives. So, never divorce Him for the sake of another.

EVERYTHING HAPPENS ACCORDING TO HIS WILL

Even though individuals have their own will, ultimately God's Will will win. Can human beings do *anything* against God's Will? No. Nothing that is against His Will will ever happen. A certain thing will happen only if God's Will okays it. Otherwise it won't. We should trust completely. If we have trust, then even if others do or say something to us, we need not have any negative feeling about them. We need not even think that they are being negative to us. They cannot be negative to us without God's Will. Why should our good God allow one person to have negative feelings against another? If that is happening, there must be some reason for it. We should not even call it a negative feeling. It is a positive feeling that seems to be hurting me, and so I call it negative. If others cause us difficulty, we call them negative people; but nobody can cause us difficulty without God's Will. That means in some way or other we deserve to face such people; so those people are simply acting as instruments of God.

God uses some people to give us an experience. It's all for our education. Rewarding and punishing both come from God, and are for our benefit. If we think that way, we won't be projecting negative vibrations toward the people who we think are negative to us. See? Even by thinking that they are negative, you are projecting a negative image. It's hard for you to love the people who project a negative image toward you, because you feel they are negative. The minute you say, "She is negative to me, but I am going to love her anyway," you are trying to force yourself to love that person. Instead, if you treat her as an instrument of God and feel, "God is doing something to me through that individual, but she is a beautiful person," then there is no negative feeling and no negative person. And it is easy for you to be loving. You don't need to force yourself to love someone.

15 October

YOUR NOT KNOWING IS THE DARKNESS

Where there is light, certainly there is darkness also. What is darkness? Absence of light. When you don't recognize the light, you see darkness. What is dark to you is bright to a cat or a tiger or a bat. It's all relative. And when you have one, you have the other also. You cannot only have one side of the coin.

But the moment that you *know* that darkness is a part of the whole, it is not darkness anymore. The real darkness lies in your ignorance of what it is. Your not knowing is the darkness. The minute you know, you respect both sides, and it's no longer darkness. Don't we respect both day and night? We *want* both day and night. Night makes the day complete.

Pleasure and pain are also two sides of the same coin. If you only want pleasure and hate pain, you become miserable. After one, the other is certain to follow. When it comes and you don't want it, you fight it. Instead, we must recognize that life is like that.

If someone is nice to you and you demand that he or she must always be nice to you, always respect you, then you are seeing only one side. If the other side comes, you deny the person, you hate the person. You should know that the other side will also be there. Love that person for the other side also. Then you are in a different light where there is no darkness at all. That is what you call Supreme Light. That Light is not like this light that casts a shadow; that Light is a shadowless Light. Once you go into that state, you still see the light and darkness, but you respect them both.

16 October

THERE IS NOTHING TERRIBLE IN THIS LIFE

You need good light to make a movie, is it not so? And then you need good darkness in which to show it. Isn't it funny? The cameraman says, "Oh, there is not enough light; we can't take the picture." But when they want to show the film, they turn off all the lights. So, what is important for a movie? Both. Light to take it, darkness to show it.

The minute you learn to respect and see both sides of the coin as equally good, you can enjoy both. You never hate anything. It is only a matter of your understanding and acceptance. Then you enjoy everything in life. Everything! There is nothing, nothing, nothing that is terrible, bad or negative in this life.

Let us have that light of understanding. Accept things as they are, people as they are. Don't demand anything. Don't put conditions: "Only when you do this does it prove that you love me." Rise above all this. Our attitude, our approach, our love should be unconditional. Simply accept people for what they are, as they are. Learn to love everyone and everyone will love you, no doubt. Then, life is worth living. The world becomes a heaven on earth for you.

17 October

WILL YOU MAKE A GOOD BABYSITTER?

Question: We have been very busy lately and we haven't been able to meditate or do *pujas* anymore. Even while at school or while playing we seem to forget about God. What can we do to bring God back into our lives?

Sri Gurudev: The easiest way is to know that whatever you do is worship. Anything that you do anywhere, even if you wash dishes to help your mama, it's a *puja*. *Puja* doesn't mean only sitting in front of an altar and doing something. The kitchen is an altar, the house is a temple, and God is in you. When you go to sleep, you are putting God to sleep. When you walk around, you are taking God in a procession. So we have to get into the habit of thinking that way. Whatever you do each day should be done as worship. If you know that, then you won't say, "I don't have time to do *puja*." That doesn't mean that you should never do *puja* as *puja*. When you have the time, do that kind of *puja* also.

God didn't create us to sit in front of Him and talk about His glories. He sent us to do some work, to serve humanity, to take care of everything and everybody. In a way, we are all God's babysitters. Each being is a child of God. Everything is God's creation. That means your puppy is a child of God. Your pussycat is a child of God. So God has created you as a babysitter for all His children. You say, "Ohh, I want to please You, God." But if you forget about all His children, and sit in front of Him and praise Him while the children cry, will you make a good babysitter? A babysitter is hired to take care of the babies. Likewise, we are created to serve everyone.

MAKE YOUR ENTIRE LIFE AN ACT OF WORSHIP

If you sit and meditate, that's good; but what are you doing the rest of the time? Are you also meditating then? Whatever you do, do it as a meditation. That is important. If you are doing your job as a meditation, you don't even need to sit and meditate. But are you able to do that? If not, then meditation is a preparation for you. When you sit for meditation, you are preparing yourself to apply that meditative attitude in all your actions.

Puja or formal worship is also like that. To make the entire life an act of worship, you begin here. You are taking a vow, "My every act should be a worship like this." It is almost like practicing at home before coming on stage. Once you are an expert dancer, you don't have to practice at home. At any time you can just get up onto the stage. Still, even the experts need a little rehearsal. That is where the *puja* comes in. A little rehearsal before you begin the day. If you don't have much time, a little time will do. It need not be elaborate. The scriptures say, "God is happy with a simple form of worship." God does not look for your formalities. God looks at your heart. He sees with what kind of heart you are worshipping.

19 October

THE TRUE CHIEF ADMINISTRATOR IS GOD

Know that you are being guided by God. Whatever situation is presented to you is presented by God. You should realize that. You may have a parent, a boss, someone who is in charge of you, but the true Chief Administrator is God and no other authority.

Do not worry about administrators or outside authorities. Just do your job as well as you can. Don't be afraid of losing your job, or of anyone or anything. To have a calm and serene mind, you must put complete trust in God. God has brought you this far, and the same God will guide you continuously.

If worldly administrators don't appreciate you, don't worry. The Chief Administrator will put you somewhere else. Remember, we are serving Him. All the rest is secondary. That confidence alone will help you. When you do things with total faith, total confidence, even the ordinary administrators will recognize and appreciate it. They will hesitate to interfere in your work. *They* will be afraid of you. Let them see your faith and the courage based on that faith in your actions. You can do that only if you develop total, implicit faith in that guidance.

DEPEND ENTIRELY ON GOD

A beautiful story in the ancient Hindu scripture, the Mahabharata, clearly teaches what is meant by real surrender to God.

A beautiful princess named Draupadi was brought to the king's court. In the ancient days when you wanted to show that you had won a victory over someone, you did something that would damage his reputation. So the king decided to put Draupadi to shame by stripping her sari off. By doing this, he would ruin Draupadi's husband's reputation.

A sari is six or seven yards of material which is gracefully wrapped around and tucked in with delicate folds. The king began to pull Draupadi's sari, and though she was clutching it tightly, very soon he succeeded in pulling out one round and almost a second round of the sari. Draupadi was so frightened; she was crying out to God, in the form of Lord Krishna. "Krishna, Krishna!" she cried, but her cries went unanswered. In another minute, the entire sari would be pulled off. Her strength could never match the king's. Realizing the situation she thought to herself, "This is the final round of my sari; if I lose this also I will be doomed. " In that moment a great realization dawned, "What am I doing? I cannot take care of myself anymore. Lord Krishna, if you want me to face this disgrace I will accept it. I totally trust you; my life is in your hands." With that she let go of the sari and held her hands up and cried, "Krishna!"

Draupadi just stood there calling and crying to Lord Krishna while the king mercilessly pulled the last round of her sari. But as he pulled, the cloth kept coming. After the last round, there was another, and another, and another. He pulled again and again, yet there seemed to be no end to the sari. He was pulling and pulling and pulling. Yards and yards and yards of sari seemed to be coming from somewhere. The King was soon exhausted and could pull no more. Draupadi was saved.

This story illustrates a great truth. Even God cannot come and help you as long as you have faith in your own strength. If you are not totally surrendered, He says, "Okay, you still have strength, then why don't you take care of yourself." Complete surrender means to give up totally and depend entirely on God.

21 October

THERE IS NO SUPERIOR OR INFERIOR WORK

In nature, every job is equally important. There is no superior or inferior work. If you feel comfortable with a job, and if you can perform it with joy, that's your work. You can perform any work with joy if you know that every job is equally good. You lose the joy of doing things when you don't understand the importance of them, when you compare your work with someone else's work. There is no blue collar work, white collar work. If you want to see it that way, your legs are doing blue collar work. Your head is doing white collar work. Is it not so? Your blue collar workers have to take the white collar worker wherever it wants to go. We are the ones who create all this superiority/inferiority. The world needs everything. Every action is equally good. Do them all with joy.

IT'S NOT WHAT YOU GATHER THAT MAKES YOU SELFISH

Question: How can we cultivate the neutrality to evaluate our own thoughts and actions, which are so close to us?

Sri Gurudev: Find out whether your own thoughts are based on selfishness or not. If your thoughts are based on selfishness, then they are always wrong. Because you are putting your own concern as your primary motive. You are not thinking of others. So naturally you will lean towards your own benefit. We have to analyze every thought, every action, with this guideline: "Am I doing it selflessly?"

This might lead to another question: "What about my eating, sleeping, having certain facilities? Is it selfish for me to buy a house?" If you are doing it just for *your* sake, then yes, it is selfish. It's not what you gather or keep with you that makes you selfish, but how you use them. Even your eating can be selfless if you are eating to get the energy to serve others.

Every action should be based on some benefit to someone. You might wonder, "Shouldn't *I* at least get *some* benefit?" You will get the most benefit if you think of the benefit of others. That's why I sometimes say the most selfless person is the most selfish person, because by being selfless you keep yourself happy and peaceful always.

IF YOU DON'T GET EVERYTHING YOU WANT, YOU ARE REALLY LUCKY

Question: I want to know God, but I keep getting attracted to relationships. If God doesn't want me to be married, why can't He help me to want only Him?

Sri Gurudev: That's what He is doing. You are beginning to feel that way now. If He had given you a partner, you wouldn't even be thinking this way, you wouldn't even worry about knowing God. Now, because He *didn't* give one to you, you are turning to Him. So God is really interested in you. When He wants to help you in every way possible, He cuts off everything that would bind you. Everything that you are attached to, He cuts. "No, no, that's not it, come to me." Do you see? Is that not help? If He were not interested in you, He would say, "All right, do anything you want." Because He's interested in you, He doesn't want you to get caught in anything else. You are really lucky that way. Oh yes. Don't ever think that you are lucky if you get everything you want. No. If you don't get what you want, then you are really lucky. That means God is taking all those things away so that you will not be distracted by them.

You should be super happy if you don't get everything you want, but it's a hard truth to swallow. In many lives you see that God has given people everything, and they don't even have time to think of Him. Doesn't the Bible say that? A camel could go through the eye of a needle before God could enter into the heart of a rich man. What do you mean by rich man? So many entanglements, so many attachments, so much accumulation. Even if God wants to get in, there's no room. So don't worry. The very fact that you are not getting any partner means that God seems to be after you.

24 October

YOU DON'T NEED TO DO ANYTHING

Everything is empty without God. Marriage, an ashram, even *sannyas*—monkhood—is empty if there is no God. Each one is trying to find that joy through different ways. To find God, you don't need to do anything. Neither taking *sannyas*, nor having a family, nor living in an ashram, nor having anything is going to bring God. The minute you know that everything is nothing but emptiness, the minute you realize that God cannot be gotten from outside by doing something, then you have God. Some marry and try to get God. Some renounce and try to get God. They all ultimately want to find that joy. We should all know that it's not by doing a certain thing or by not doing a certain thing that you are going to achieve this. It is the attitude in the mind, not the state or position. It doesn't matter what you are, what you do. It's the knowledge. That's why whether it is a renounced life or a married life is immaterial. Learn to keep your peace.

YOU MUST DO ALL THAT YOU CAN TO ATTRACT THAT PERSON

If you want God, what should you do? Simply sit and cry? No. You should serve Him. If you really want to attract somebody, if you want to get somebody's love, you must serve that person. You must do all that you can to attract that person so he or she will love you. You give everything, even your life, to that person. It's also like that with God. God is here in the form of humanity, in the form of nature. So you say, "I am ready to give anything and everything in the name of God." Serve, serve, serve. That doesn't mean you just simply go, sit in a corner and cry.

Serving God is loving God. By serving and loving, you get His Grace. You make Him love you. A devotee is not a useless person simply sitting and crying. He serves everybody, everything in the name of God. Serving and loving are the ways to attain God. What is God? Who is that? Peace of mind is God. So you are ready to renounce anything and everything to retain your peace, and that is God. You can never maintain that peace if you are running after things, if you are looking for that peace outside. God is in you in the form of peace and joy.

YOU DON'T HAVE TO FEEL GUILTY

Question: How can I know when to serve others and when it is best for me to say no without guilt?

Sri Gurudev: You yourself should know how much you can give. You cannot give beyond your capacity. If you have done a lot of service that day, and if you are really tired, you should say no. Otherwise you are saying no to your own body or mind. In the name of helping others, you should not put your body into a situation where it might get hurt. Your conscience will tell you if you are just finding an excuse; but if you really need the rest, then you can honestly say no. You don't have to feel guilty about it.

Why should you feel guilty? Nobody expects you to go beyond your capacity. If you try to do something beyond your capacity, you might even make a mess of it. So, know your capacity, know your limitations. Then offer your services. There's no need to feel guilty at all. If you feel guilty, then maybe you can do it but you just don't want to. If your conscience is clear, you don't have to feel guilty.

Ask advice from your own pure Self. Your conscience is always clean. That's the part of God in you. It's what you call the guru within. It's not necessary to always get advice from someone outside. The conscience is constantly giving us advice, but often we don't listen to it. We don't even want to listen. Someone else can only help you for a while. You should learn to ask that buddy within. Sometimes you might feel a conflict: "I don't know which is the Self and which is the ego. One says, 'Do it;' the other says, 'Don't do it.'" In that case go to someone who is capable of recognizing the difference. But ultimately we have to develop the capacity to discriminate within ourselves. That is why meditation is so important. Until you become established in that, at least in meditation you should be able to hear your own inner Self.

27 October

GOD IS NEUTRAL

Question: You have said that God is neutral. You have also said He can approve or disapprove of our plans and intentions. Please explain how both can be true.

Sri Gurudev: When I said that God is neutral, that was true. And when I said that He approves and disapproves, that was also true. The sun's rays don't have any color, it's true. But when those same rays pass through a prism, you see all the seven colors; isn't that also true? So you see things in a different light depending upon whether you are looking from this side of the prism or that side of the prism. Either one could be true, because absolute Truth is totally different. The mind can never grasp the absolute Truth because the mind itself is limited. If the mind wants to grasp something, it colors it according to its own state. So you can see God as someone who is supervising everything, or as someone who is approving and disapproving, like your conscience.

Your conscience is that part of God that is within you. It doesn't approve of everything that you want to do. God would disapprove just as your conscience does, but He won't stop you if you still want to do it. In that way, He is neutral. The light from the sun is there. In that light, you might see a big ditch in the road. If, after seeing the ditch, you close your eyes and walk, will the sun come and stop you? No. The sun showed you the ditch, but it won't stop you from falling in. What you do about the ditch is your business. In that way God is neutral. God just presents the facts and allows you to listen or to not listen. Then you face whatever comes. In the absolute sense, God is not doing anything; but that can be experienced only when you transcend the mind and get beyond its limitations. Until then, we just have to understand it as "my will," and "God's Will."

28 October

IT IS THE TEACHINGS

Question: When the master is not physically present, how can the disciple be sure that he or she is following the master's guidance?

Sri Gurudev: If you just look within, "What would my master tell me if he or she were right here sitting in front of me?", you will get the answer. "Yes, he has spoken about that many times. I know what he would say to me." Then follow it; you have the master, or the spiritual guide, or the guru there. The guru is not just the physical body; it is the teachings. Even if you don't have a guru, even if you have no one to advise you, if you learn to listen within, your own conscience will guide you. The guru is not a person somewhere. Your conscience always tells you what is right and what is wrong. That is the guru within. Listen to that, and follow it.

NOBODY CAN REPLACE YOU

Divine Will has no tinge of selfishness. Ego means selfishness, "I," "me," "I am doing it for *my* sake." So whatever you will to do for your sake is egoistic and will have its own return. We have to face it. But without the ego, we would say, "Some Cosmic Power makes me work. The God in me motivates me. He sent me here and He is making me do everything. I am an instrument. He gave me everything. He may take it all back. Nothing belongs to me. Not even the body belongs to me." We should perform all our actions with this feeling, free from egoism. That is Divine Will. Your conscience prompts you, not the ego. The conscience will always say, "It's good for everybody." Don't even pray, "Let *me* be happy. Help *me*. Make *me* good." Always think in terms of the cosmos: *"Sarveshaam swastir bhavatu."*—"May *all* be happy." So, keep on dinning it into the mind, "Thy Will be done. It's all for Jesus, all for Moses, all for Buddha, all for Allah." Use any name, it doesn't matter. "All for the Ashram. All for the Cosmic Consciousness. Nothing for me. I'm not even eating for my sake. I am eating because I have to serve." That should be the thought behind our every act. The minute you begin to live that way, your life will be totally, totally different. You will enjoy supreme joy. You will not be affected by these petty little things.

We should always roar like lions, "I am that I am! I am ever joyful, ever peaceful! None of this nonsense will affect me!" We must have that strength and courage. Even if you *act* temporarily, "I am a super yogi!" for one week, you will see the difference. It's not just to be read, or heard or preached. It should be lived. And you *can* live that life. Don't say, "Oh, that is only fit for saints. I am just an ordinary person." You are not ordinary. If you were ordinary, you wouldn't even be here. Nobody is ordinary here. No. Even a thorn has a purpose. It has been placed here for a particular cause and it is unique in its place. Nothing can be substituted for that. Nobody can replace you. You are unique in your position. Don't try to compare yourself with others. You are all-important. Everybody is needed in this cosmos. Be proud of your existence.

30 October

PLAY, PLAY, PLAY

The origin of thought is the Cosmic Mind itself, which we call God. It is God who thought of creating. Since then, thoughts are here. As long as there is mind, there will be thoughts. The mind is nothing but a bundle of thoughts. Even the idea of working toward the thoughtless state itself is a thought: "I want to be thoughtless." It's not that we are trying to do away with the thoughts. What we want is to have the right thoughts, ones that would not disturb the mind. Thoughts are of two kinds: working thoughts and playing thoughts. In working thoughts, you get tensed up, you become anxious. In playing thoughts, you are relaxed. So convert all of your thoughts into playing thoughts. Play while you work. Let it be a continuous play. There is nothing else you should be doing in your life. Just play, play, play.

ADAPT, ADJUST, ACCOMMODATE; BEAR INSULT, BEAR INJURY

It is easy to sit and meditate. The most difficult part is to practice bearing insult and injury, learning to adapt, adjust and accommodate. These are the teachings of the great saint and sage of the Himalayas, Sri Swami Sivanandaji Maharaj. You can do your prayer, meditation, spiritual practices all by yourself. But what about your attitude when you deal with people, when you work with them day in and day out? That is where you have to prove that you have achieved something in your spiritual practices.

If a person practices adapting, adjusting and accommodating, he would never point a finger at others and blame them. Even if another person is at fault, if you know how to adapt, adjust and accommodate, you are able to rise above those situations. Still, the most difficult thing is to bear insult and injury. That needs a tremendous capacity to keep the mind totally under your thumb.

Do your daily work, deal with everyone, move with everybody. Be in the ocean, but learn to surf well.

November

1 November

THAT IS WHAT YOU CALL SPIRITUAL EXPERIENCE

Living together happily as one beautiful family with total love is God. People still ask me, "What is it that I have been doing all these years? I have been practicing, but I haven't realized God, I haven't had any experience." I don't know what experience it is that they want. They want to be lifted up from the floor a few inches? Or have some hallucinations? To me, even if you experience such things, it's still nonsense. That's not the spiritual experience I would want. Yes, you might have some visions, you might see some lights, hear some sounds, all right. What is the benefit that those things bring to others? The real experience is to move around with a smiling face, a loving face. That is spiritual: to see the spirit in others, to love everybody. To rise above these differences of the lower nature.

Real spiritual experience brings harmony. What is the use of those other experiences if you can't live comfortably, harmoniously, lovingly with ten people? Everybody should love you. To me that is what you call spiritual experience. Keep that in mind. "I will live a life that will make everybody love me. Nobody should look at me with even a little dismay." Only if you can do that, are you growing spiritually. All other things are just nonsense. Even your spiritual practices.

2 November

IN THE SAME WAY, YOU BRUSH YOUR HEART ALSO

You may be regular in your practice; but if every morning you sit without any movement for one whole hour and meditate, and the next minute you go out and express all your negative feelings to others, what is the use? That's not spiritual practice. How much of animosity, backbiting, dislike, hatred, "I don't like her, I don't like him," is there in your life? Touch your own heart and question yourself, "Am I loved by everyone? Do I love everyone? Or is there any dislike towards anybody?" Go to that person, shake his or her hand and say, "I'm sorry I had this kind of feeling. It's terrible, it makes me sick. I am sorry." That is worth a hundred days' meditation. Have no ill feeling toward anyone. The moment you have some difference of opinion or any feelings of suspicion, go, immediately talk to that person. Say, "I am getting a feeling like this. Please, I must clarify it. Come on, let's get that over with." Don't even allow it to stay in your heart for a few hours. Sometimes these kinds of feelings come up. It's natural; but don't go to sleep like that. Before you go to bed, it should be cleared up. Don't you brush your teeth before you go to bed? You go to bed with clean teeth, is it not so? In the same way, brush your heart also. How can you brush your heart? Talk to the people concerned. Clean out the negative feelings, then you can go to bed with a clean heart and sleep comfortably. If you consciously try it, it becomes very easy. It's not really an impossible thing.

3 November

WHATEVER YOU DO, DO IT PEACEFULLY, GENTLY

Question: I want to help end the nuclear arms race around the world. Do you think it's important to join a freeze group? Or can one person accomplish more through meditation, prayer and chanting?

Sri Gurudev: I would say prayer, chanting and meditation would be more helpful. If you still want to join a group, all right; but don't become a radical. Don't create more violence in trying to remove violence. You can join hands, but whatever you do, do it peacefully, gently. And if you can't find a group like that, do it yourself. Think, send your prayers. Sincere, heartfelt prayers will spread out all over the globe, and all those who are ready will receive them. More than anything else, know that you are just doing your part, but ultimately it's all in the hands of the One who created the world. He knows how to handle it. You are simply playing a small part.

4 November

JUST BE CONTENTED

Question: I feel a strong desire to be a mother and part of a family unit, yet I haven't met a man to begin this family with. I sometimes become impatient and anxious, begin to lack faith and trust, and feel pressured because of my age. Do you have any suggestions?

Sri Gurudev: God has a purpose for having you here, but you may want to do something of your own. If God really wanted you to get married and have a family, even if you didn't want it, somebody would have come and kidnapped you. Sometimes we want many things, but the Higher Will says, "It's not good for you. I have not created you for that purpose." Or, "You are not ready for it." You might say, "No, I am thirty-three. I am ready." Well, to God maybe you are still a thirty-three month old baby. You think you are ready but God still says no. We sometimes think that we all should be doing the same thing. That is not so. It is that Cosmic Consciousness, which we call God, that created everything and everybody for a certain purpose. The purpose need not be the same for everyone. He functions through all the people to fulfill His cosmic mission. Maybe you are supposed to do something without getting into family life. By not accepting that, you are not fulfilling your duty as a single person; neither are you getting into family life as you wanted. So you are losing both. You are neither following God's Will, nor following your will. You are revolting against God: "I don't want to be like that. I want to be like this." And God is not allowing you to be the way you want. When you don't want to be that and God doesn't want you to be this, it's a constant fight.

We all have some purpose to fulfill. You are unique in your place. Just be contented, "God has created me for some purpose. Let me fulfill whatever it is. Even if I don't know what I am doing." If you ask God, He will say, "I have a purpose for you. Just wait. I don't need to be using everybody, every day, all the time." So just be contented. If God wants a grandson, He will certainly send some nice fellow to you. He will send you whatever you need to fulfill that purpose.

5 November

IT'S STILL A DRY LEAF

Speak less and only speak about what is to be spoken of. Control of the tongue is very important. The tongue does two things: tasting and talking. Have limitations in both. Speak less, speak softly and speak the truth. Occasionally stay away from talking completely and experience silence.

By talking we expose our ignorance and create a lot of enemies. It's not easy to talk and still be respected. If it were my choice, I would prefer to be silent. But then I think, "Why should I be silent? Am *I* talking? No. Someone makes me talk, and I talk. If He makes me keep quiet, I will keep quiet." That's all. When you have this feeling, the talking is not *your* talking. You are just a speaker, and somebody else is talking through it. So you don't need to worry about that.

Don't have any want of your own. Whatever has to happen through you, let it happen. If you are made to talk, talk. If you are made to sleep, sleep. If you are made to eat, eat. Then you don't need to worry about any of these things.

Resign yourself completely into the hands of God, into the hands of the unseen power that functions through you. You will be contented. "This is where you placed me. I am here. Tomorrow you may throw me into the ditch, I will be happy there also." Like a dry leaf. Suppose the wind comes and the leaf gets carried up and dropped on the top of a church. If another gust comes and it is thrown on top of a manure pile, then what? It's still a dry leaf. No matter where it lands, it just says, "Well, You are the one who placed me here, fine. Maybe You have a purpose for that." That's what you call total acceptance. Trust in God; then all of life will be joyful and peaceful.

6 November

HOW MANY OF YOU WOULD TELL THE TRUTH?

Question: Can a little lie told to a person be loving and actually prevent hurt?

Sri Gurudev: Well, I have a philosophy about that. What is a lie? Is a lie something terrible? Is it always bad to lie? If so, why should there even be such a thing as a lie at all in this universe? Why has lying been created? Lying by itself is not bad. You can lie under certain conditions. If it is going to produce at least some benefit to somebody and no harm to anybody, then even a lie is the truth. In the same way, don't think that your own golden truth is always wonderful. Sometimes truth can be more terrible than lying. Would you like an example?

Once upon a time there lived a *sadhu*—a wandering mendicant—in a remote wooded area. He lived in a nice, small hut. One fine day a young, beautiful girl who was wearing all kinds of nice jewels, diamonds, rubies and what not, came running up to him. "Swami, please help me." He was startled to see the young girl. She said, "Please, somebody is chasing me to rob me of all these things. He may even kill me. Please let me hide somewhere." And without even waiting for his permission, she just ran into the hut and hid herself in a corner. Within a few minutes, a terrible looking man with a nice dagger in his hand came running by. "Hey, *sadhu*. Did a young girl come by here?" *Sadhus* should not tell lies, isn't it so? What should he say? The truth and nothing but the truth? How many of you would tell the truth? Probably not even one.

The *sadhu* said, "What? What do you mean by that? Why would a young girl come here? Don't you see that I am a *sadhu* and this is a hermitage? This is no place for young girls." "Oh, so you didn't see anyone?" "Why are you looking for a young girl here? I am just an old man living in a forest." Did he tell the truth? No. So, it's a lie, in a way. He didn't say, "No;" he just questioned the man. And by doing so, he saved 3 lives: the life of the girl, his own life, and the life of the thief. The thief was ready to kill the girl to get the jewels; then he would have had to kill the *sadhu* who would have been a witness; and the police would have caught the thief and put him to death.

So don't worry about whether something is the truth or a lie. Think about what the outcome of it is. Always look at the outcome of your actions and the motive with which you perform them. The *sadhu* was not really cheating the man by that lie; in fact, he saved that man's life by preventing the crime. He wished well for him, so his lie had a good intention and a beautiful outcome. That's how we should think. In that sense, there is nothing bad in this whole universe.

ALL THE BEAUTY QUEENS, WHERE ARE THEY NOW?

Realize that nothing is yours. You didn't come with anything and you are not going to go with anything. Things were given to you along the way. At a certain period things and people came to you. At a certain period, they might go again. It's all just a carnival. We meet people and sit with them on a carousel for a while. Your neighbor might be sitting on a tiger, you might be sitting on a horse. You say, "Hey, hello," and go around in a circle. When the ride is over you get down, but he may still continue. Or he may get down and go somewhere else. Just think of the whole thing as a carnival. We just meet people; and as long as we are together we say hello to each other and try to be nice, try to be useful.

Nothing belongs to us. So what is this "mine, mine, mine" business? Many "mines" bring many explosions. Don't identify yourself with your possessions. How many ex-millionaires are paupers now? How many great men who once ruled countries are now begging? What is permanent? Think about all these things. All the beauty queens, where are they now? What is there to be egotistical about?

Not only individuals, but even as a country, we have that pride. What are we so proud of? Nothing is ours. Who knows, one day there may not be even a trace left. Be prepared for anything. Do not be attached to things. If they come, let them come. It's all God's business, part of nature's plan. So remembering these things will take our pride away. We'll learn to be humble. It's always better to be humble, with our feet on the ground, so we don't fall. If you try to rise up and you slip, you will have a terrible fall. The person who is sitting on the floor need not be worried about falling down.

8 November

SMILE AT HIM

Question: In order to overcome my fear of being beaten up, I am learning how to fight. Is this the proper course?

Sri Gurudev: First of all, let me remind you that however well you might learn to fight, there will always be a better fighter than you. You may not be beaten up by a classmate, but there will be a stronger man outside of the school. And when you learn to fight, you first think of defending yourself. But later on when you really learn well, and there is nobody to defend yourself from, then you will want to exhibit your capacity. Isn't it so? Otherwise why should you learn? When you have something, you want to show it off. Learning to fight is not going to help you in defending yourself or in any other way. The best way to defend yourself is with your mental poise and courage. Why is somebody going to beat you up? Think about it. Why should he beat you? Maybe he had some grudge against you. He thinks of you as an enemy. Find out the cause. If there is some fault on your side, go, apologize, make him your friend. You might say, "No, no, no, it's just a man on the road, some crazy fellow." If you are really innocent, you will send out a beautiful, innocent vibration. He may come near you, but he will forget to attack you. So the best defense is to keep a clean and serene mind; smile at him. If he still wants to come and hit you, you should have the courage to say, "Yes, if you like to do it and if you think that you are going to enjoy it, do it. I am ready to make you happy. Is that what you want? Do it." He will never touch you then.

9 November

YOU ARE REALLY GIVING A BETTER LESSON

When Lord Jesus said, "If somebody slaps you on one cheek, show the other cheek also," what did that mean? By showing the other cheek you are really giving the person a better lesson. You make him feel ashamed of what he has done. If you return another slap, you are only beating his body. If you follow this advice of Jesus, you are beating the mind, the ego.

It takes more courage and strength to smile at a person who hates you than to hit back. It is here that the idea of karma can be helpful. If somebody just comes and hits you for no reason, stop and think to yourself, "Probably this is my karma. I must have hit somebody sometime in the past and escaped from getting hit or being punished for it. Now this person is returning what I gave out." Accept it. Certainly there is no effect without a cause. Nobody can come and hurt you if you are really that innocent. When somebody suddenly hits you, he is just giving you what you failed to receive from the other person to whom you gave something. You should thank him. "You have helped me to purge this karma at last. Thank you so much." At the same time you are teaching him a lesson. So this is the best way to do it. Fighting is never going to stop another fight. Only love, not more hatred, will heal hatred.

10 November

GO TO THEM WITH ALL COURAGE

Question: Before I believed, I created much bad karma in this life. Now I am frightened most of the time about how I must pay it back. How can I handle this fear?

Sri Gurudev: Your fear is unnecessary. We all make mistakes. Once you realize that you have made a mistake, repent. Learn the lessons from the mistakes that you make. Failures are stepping stones to future success. If you are going to brood over your past mistakes and be afraid that something terrible will happen, you will just waste your time. Nothing will happen. Nature's grace is such that it will pardon any mistake, because only by mistakes do you learn. If a child is going to think of all the falls it had while it was learning to walk, it will never walk. So treat the falls as stepping stones.

If you have the opportunity to see the people you wronged, go to them with all courage and apologize. Say, "I made a mistake. I was a fool. I was ignorant. I didn't know what I was doing. Please excuse me." That is the only way to repay your debts. If you cannot see these people, if they are not here anymore, at least mentally pray for them. Think of them. Send your apologies to them. That way you can pay them back and it won't affect you.

11 November

IT'S ALL GOD'S WILL

Question: Often we willfully break the commandments of the scriptures. How can this be God's Will?

Sri Gurudev: It *is* all God's Will. It is God's Will that you asked me this question, and it is God's Will that is going to answer you. Ultimately, that is the truth. Nothing, nothing, nothing, happens without God's Will. All the holy scriptures say that; but when will you realize it? When you go ahead and do certain things as *your* will and learn the lessons from the consequences. Then you say, "Well, I tried to use my will. Now I realize that it's all His Will ultimately."

12 November

YOUR PRAYER SHOULD BE TO GIVE THEM UNDERSTANDING

Question: If we pray for others, is their karma taken away?

Sri Gurudev: We are not praying to have the karma of others taken away. We pray so that they can get insight into their karma and get the strength to face it and purge it out. Your prayer should be for their strength and understanding. What you sow, you must reap. If they understand the cause and the benefit of the suffering, then they can easily bear it. Just because you say, "Take their karma away," God is not going to listen to you and take their karma away. So a prayer should help them to understand.

13 November

MANY, MANY THINGS CAN HAPPEN THROUGH PRAYER

When you pray, you send out healing vibrations and good thoughts into the cosmos. They circulate there. If you pray for a particular individual, no matter where that individual is, your thought forms go there and reach that person. The person may not even know that you are praying for his or her welfare, but will be able to receive it and be helped. Sometimes your prayers are universal; in that case, those who have an open sail will catch it. But you can personalize it also, and it will certainly be received.

If a person's karma is strong and your prayer is not that strong, you cannot even penetrate into it. Then what is the use of praying? When others know that so many people are praying for them, it will give them comfort. And even if some people do not want your prayer, you can still pray. By praying for others, you get the benefit yourself, because you are opening up your own heart. You are showing your compassionate side. Your mind gets purified when you pray for others. You become a better person. Through your prayer you are expressing your faith in God.

It is not that karma can be alleviated or even eradicated by prayers. Instead, your prayers act as an anaesthesia so that the person doesn't go through the operation with pain.

In numerous ways, prayer certainly helps. It is a powerful, powerful practice. Many, many things can happen by prayer. Radical minds may not accept or understand it. But a sincere prayer that comes from a faithful heart can perform miracles. So have that faith. Pray for yourself, pray for others. You will certainly purify your heart.

14 November

DON'T EVEN RUN AFTER GOD

Be a good person, do good things, be happy, be peaceful. Don't allow your peace and joy to get ruined, not even in the name of God. If He doesn't want to come to you, let Him do what He is supposed to be doing. You don't need to go and beg Him. When you are ready, He will come.

Yes. Stop running after God and He will run after you. Tell Him, "Mr. God, I'm not very keen about looking for You. I know when I am ready You will come to me. Just take Your time." The mere anxiety in looking for God itself will disturb your mind. Not wanting anything means that you don't even want God. Stay away from all the wants. Then all the things you once wanted will want you, including God. Remember that. Don't ever, ever run after anything or anybody, including God. Stay where you are and say, "I am content, I am happy to be what I am. If anything comes to me, let it come in its own time. I am not in a hurry. I'm not going to run after anything."

That is what you call contentment. Contentment is purity of heart, not a heart that is anxiously searching for something. When you have that contentment, everything is golden to you. Gradually learn to rise above all your wants. Keep your body and mind totally easeful and peaceful. Let things come and go as nature wants, as God wants. There is a Cosmic Awareness that will function through you. Don't put your ego in the middle and create an impediment for that Awareness to function through. We create a lot of impediments along the way.

15 November

WHOEVER IS INTERESTED IN REALITY IS AN ISRAELITE

Question: As a child I learned a basic Jewish prayer, "Hear, O Israel! The Lord is our God, the Lord is One." Please explain what this means?

Sri Gurudev: The meaning is very clear here. I don't think it's just the name of a country. Israel is what is real. And whoever thinks of that reality and works to realize the reality are the chosen people. They may be living in Africa, or Australia, or Himalayan cave or Katmandu, it doesn't matter. Whoever is interested in reality is an Israelite. So this song is addressed to the true children of that absolute reality: "Hear, O children of the reality! The Lord is our God." There is only one God who is our Lord, who is the life in us. We are of that image. God is always one. Every religion talks about this.

WHO IS GREAT?

I'm sure you must have had at least a glimpse of God, otherwise you would not even be reading a book like this. Unfortunately, we seldom see that reflection of God inside, which is in you *as* you. The duty of the spiritual teacher is to act as a mirror to show you the Light within. And it is the Light within that helps you to realize God. That Light does not shine just within a few individual sages or saints. If you care to learn, you can learn from anything and everything. A speck of dust can teach you something. A plant can teach you something. A seed can teach you something. A worm can teach you something. A bird, a beast, a stone. You can learn something from a thief. If you really want to learn, everything can teach you. The unfortunate thing is that everyone wants to teach, no one wants to learn.

Sage Thiruvalluvar says, "Who is great? The one who does what is not easy." Anybody can do everyday things: find a little food and a little shelter, build a family, have a little fun. There is no greatness in it. Many people do that. Even animals do that. So what should we do that is difficult? Know the Truth. It is for that sake you need the help of someone who has already seen the Light.

17 November

I DON'T NEED TO BE AFRAID OF ANYONE IN THIS WORLD

Question: Would you please say something about fear? Sometimes I wake up at night and do not know who or where I am, except that my heart is pounding because I am so frightened.

Sri Gurudev: The part that sleeps in a sleeping state is the conscious mind. The subconscious mind can still function. When the conscious mind sleeps and the subconscious mind functions, you call it a dream. If the subconscious mind also sleeps, that is what you call sleep. When the conscious mind sleeps, the fear that is in the subconscious mind takes the opportunity to come to the surface. Probing into that fear is almost like analyzing the garbage before throwing it out.

Instead of worrying about what caused the fear, replace it with something positive. Say, "Whatever it is, it's something that happened before. I'm not going to worry about it. It's not going to affect me anymore. I am bold, I am strong. I am consciously doing the right things. I am practicing yoga. I am doing a lot of prayer and meditation. I trust in God. I love everybody. I don't need to be afraid of anyone in this world because all people are my brothers and sisters. Everyone is my own Self." See? Din the positive thoughts into the subconscious mind with the conscious mind. Consciously work at it. When the positive thoughts go in, they will squeeze the undesirable thoughts out of the subconscious. Modern psychology seems to be interested in probing into it, "What caused it? Is it your father, mother?" Yoga doesn't worry about that. Ignore it. The more you think about it, the more you are encouraging it. The more you think about a thought, the more it gets strengthened. Any thought. If you ignore it, you are starving it. By putting in positive thoughts, the fear will go away.

18 November

WEAR THE MANTRAM AS YOUR ARMOR

Question: Would you please give us some advice for what to do during those times when we are more aware of the devil inside?

Sri Gurudev: Be careful. Watch every one of your actions. At the same time, look for help. The devil is powerful, no doubt. You cannot handle him by yourself. If you say, "I can win over him," you might fail. So it's at such times that you say, "God, I cannot do it by myself. I need Your help." Think of God more. Pray sincerely, repeat your mantram more. If the devil knows that you are calling for help, he won't just stand there. He knows that you are calling somebody greater than himself. He knows that he is in trouble. He wants to save his life.

The mantram is your help. Shout it. The mantram is your protection and a shield around you. Wear the mantram as your armor. There's no greater power than that. It's the devil against the Divine. But you must have that kind of confidence. If you don't have that confidence and you still shout, the devil knows that. You should be totally, totally confident in what you are doing. The devil can read your mind. He knows how strongly you are calling. How sincere you are. If you have faith even the size of a mustard seed, you can move mountains.

19 November

LET IT BE ALWAYS IN YOUR HEART AND ON YOUR LIPS

Be very regular in your chanting and mantra repetition. That is the most important practice. Even if you miss other things, don't ever miss the mantra repetition. Let it be a part and parcel of your life. The mantram literally surrounds you. The mantram acts as a shield around you. No undesirable influence can affect you. When you take a trip begin by repeating the mantram. When you drive, keep repeating the mantram. In every available situation, let it be always in your heart and on your lips. You will see miracles happening. But it all depends upon how sincere you are and how devoted you are to it.

20 November

IT WILL ALL BE TOTALLY TAKEN CARE OF

By repetition of a mantram alone, many hundreds of great saints have experienced Divine Consciousness. Knowing the meaning of the mantram is not even necessary. The faith behind it is more important. Whatever mantram is given to you, or whichever one you choose, stick to that one and have complete faith in it. Keep practicing. All the mantrams are equally good. Repeat the mantram consciously until your system takes over and repeats it unconsciously. Very soon you will realize how happy and healthy and peaceful you can be. A mantram can take care of physical health, mental problems, everything. It will all be totally taken care of by the mantram alone.

21 November

THE BEST COMFORTER IS INSIDE

Question: Why do we want so much to be loved, instead of just being contented to love others? Why do we crave emotional comfort and want others to care about us?

Sri Gurudev: Because we still have not realized that there is somebody in us, always, who is caring for us every minute, who is loving us every minute. If we realize that, why do we want somebody else to love us? In a way, the more you look for somebody else to love you, the more you might not get that love. Failing to get love from outside yourself may actually be helpful, because ultimately it will make you turn inward and say, "Nobody seems to be loving me. God, You are the only one to love me." If others love you, you will forget God. "God, I am happy with that person. I don't need to worry about You now." Yes, when everything fails you turn to God. In a way, God seems to really be loving you. That's the very reason He doesn't want anybody to love you or doesn't want you to go looking for love anywhere else. He is helping you to turn toward Him. If we feel that Presence in us, where is the need for any other comfort? The best Comforter is inside. All other kinds of comfort are temporary. They come, and there will be a time when they must go. Don't depend on something that comes from outside. Outside things are never going to make you happy. And it *should* be that way, so that one day you will realize that there is always someone to love and comfort us inside.

22 November

BECOME A FRIEND

You don't *make* a friend. You become a friend. Then you automatically will have friends. If you relate to people in a very friendly, affectionate way, by loving and caring, sharing and helping, then naturally they will see you as a good friend. When they see you as a good friend, then they become your friends. It begins with you. You should always try to do something nice for people. Never hurt anyone's feelings. The secret is to always look for opportunities to help others; look for ways to be nice to them. Sometimes they might even be nasty to you; if so, ignore it, forget it. Maybe that is the way they are; but *we* should be nice to them. Even if someone says, "Oh, you're a fool," you should say, "Thank you." Don't retaliate with the same kind of words. Soon they will get tired of all that. Afterwards, they will even feel ashamed. The great sage Thiruvalluvar said that if people do something wrong to you or hurt you, do something really good for them in return. That is the best punishment. Why? Because they will be so embarrassed to have done that to you.It is in our hands. We can always make friends with anyone and everyone if we have the right attitude. If we have the patience and understanding.

23 November

THEY LOVE YOU

If a person cannot be loving with his parents, he's not going to be loving with God either. But at the same time, you come across very hard parents who don't want to understand their children. To such parents I say, "Open up a little. The world has changed. If he is happy and contented with what you have given, why would he be running away? There's nothing wrong in his wanting to expand, to learn more. Don't you want him to be happy? He is growing in the right direction. If you really love him, let him go." But whatever happens, no seeker, no young person should ever hate his or her parents; you will never grow by hating.

You should try and try and try to get the blessings of the parents for your spiritual growth. Try your best. Sometimes if the parents are really against your spiritual pursuit, tell them, "All right, Mom, Dad, if you really don't want me to follow that, would you prefer for me to go to nightclubs and drink or take drugs? Then will you be happy?" Ask them. "Oh, no, we don't want you to do that." "Then why can't you allow me to do this? What is the use of both of us being unhappy? Let me say goodbye to you." There comes a time when the truth reveals itself. There will be a beautiful reunion. It has happened in many cases. But don't give up hope. The parents always want the best for your welfare. They love you. I have never seen any parents who would want to see their children ruined. No. Others perhaps, but not the father and mother.

24 November

NEVER FORGET A GOOD ACT

There is a beautiful saying in the Thirukkural: "We should never forget a good act that has been done to us." At the same time, it talks about the act that we should forget. That is the one that is not so good, the one that might have hurt us. We should forget it immediately. We should not even remember it for the next hour. Then we will not have anybody as an enemy. Why do we call someone an enemy? Because we remember the harm that might have been done to us. If we forget it, there won't be any enemy, is it not so? Enemies are created by our remembering what harm has been done to us. We create our enemies by remembering their misdeeds. If we have forgotten that, and if we remember all of the good deeds, even if somebody *wants* to be our enemy, he cannot because we see him as our friend. No one is one hundred percent good or one hundred percent bad. People do many good things. Maybe once in a while, because of their lower nature, they might do something bad also. But if we are going to always remember the bad things, we will keep them as our enemies, which is not good. Instead, remember the nice things that they have done; then they will always be our friends.

YOU SHOULD SEE THAT EVERYTHING IS THANKFUL TO YOU

On Thanksgiving Day, we thank the Lord for providing us with all our needs. We should be thankful always; but if we forget, then at least this one day should be kept aside especially for that. All of the nicest things that we have come from God. God has provided us with everything. Even our bodies, our intelligence. The earth on which we live. The plants, the seeds, the food, the fruit. God has given us everything. Nature and God are one and the same. Nature is another name for God. So sometimes if you don't feel comfortable with the name "God," you can say, "Nature provided everything." We should be thankful to the Nature; is it not so? We should be thankful to the Mother Nature, Mother Earth, Mother Sky, Mother Rain, Mother Wind.

Thanksgiving Day is a special day to remember to be thankful *always* for all the things we have. Not just to God, but to everyone. We always give and take, give and take, give and take; therefore we should be thankful to each other, and to each and every thing in Nature. And ultimately to that one great power, the one great intelligence that we call God. It's not possible for us to return in kind all that we get from Nature. How can we fulfill our obligation? It's impossible. The only way is to remember and to be grateful.

Not only should we be thankful to everything, but everything should be thankful to us also. We should see that all the things are thankful to us by behaving properly, treating them well. We should see that we don't hurt anyone, we don't harm anyone, or anything. Let all those beings be thankful to us also. Everything. Even your book, for example. If you throw the book aside, the book won't thank you. If you take good care of the book, read it gently, and close it gently, see that the covers are well kept, then the book also will be thanking you.

So, let us keep this idea in our life and see that we always give thanks to others, and see also that others would thank us for our proper behavior.

LIFE SHOULD HAVE CHALLENGES

If you really want to overcome any feelings of negativity, think of the people who are not as fortunate as you. Many, many others are facing more and greater challenges. When you see that, you will feel that you are very lucky in what you have. Remember that ultimately there is one source, one power. If you trust in that completely and do what you can, help comes, strength comes, courage comes. God takes care of everything and everybody.

Life *should* have challenges. Without challenges it would be a bore. It is only in challenging situations that you really learn. Never give up hope. If the mind is strong, anything can be achieved.

27 November

AM I NOT HIS BELOVED?

As spiritual seekers, we don't need to be bound by our karma, bound by these planets, astrology, this and that. We should know, "I am seeking the help from the highest One. Day by day, I am coming closer and closer and closer to God. I completely trust in God. Nothing can happen to me." You may say, "But, things *do* happen to me." They happen because you don't have that kind of faith. If things happen even with such faith, then say, "Yes, God is making it happen for my benefit." Accept it. "My Lord is giving me these experiences for my benefit. Maybe it has to be that way. I have to go through that. I have to be rubbed and scrubbed." If you have that kind of trust, everything is easy. If not, it's very difficult. That's why, if there is one quality a seeker must have, it is unshakable faith. If you have faith, you don't need to worry about anything; you will be given the strength to accept everything: "I believe in Him. I have given myself into His hands. Whatever happens happens because He allows it to happen. And it's for my good. If it were not for my good, why would He allow it to happen? Is He not powerful? Am I not His beloved?" That's what you call true devotion. True faith in God.

THE WORD IS GOD

You don't have to think of the meaning to meditate on OM. Just simply repeat OM. "OM, OM, OM, OM." When you repeat OM you hear your own sound. When you close your eyes and say, "OM, OM, OM, OM," you will be hearing your own sound, is it not? So listen to that sound. Don't think of anything else. If any other thought comes, bring the mind back. Try to listen to OM. If I speak to you, you listen to me. You hear my words, is it not so? In the same way, you can hear your own words. The word here is OM. Say OM, OM, OM, OM. See? You can hear that, no? That's good. That's enough. That is the best way to meditate on OM. You don't have to worry about such things as, "What is it, why is it, how is it?" You don't have to think *about* it. Just think of that sound. Think of the sound that OM produces. Dwell on the sound of OM itself.

The sound is not different from God. What is God? God is sound. The Bible says God is the Word. The Word is God. So God and Word are not different. In the same way, God and OM are not different. When you say, "OM, OM," God is talking to you, humming to you. Listen to that. Like a baby listens to the music of the lullaby sung by its mother. It listens to that and slowly goes to heaven. In the same way, the mind will hear OM and slowly become absorbed into that. You don't have to think about anything. Otherwise you are thinking, not meditating.

The best meditation is not to think of anything. Yes, simply OM, OM, OM, OM, OM, OM, OM. If you like it, try it.

A MANTRAM IS NOTHING BUT GOD

God has no form as such, but the scriptures say that God manifests as sound. "In the beginning, was the Word." A mantram is a sacred word; so by repeating the mantram, you are in direct communication with God, with that higher energy. When you feel that, you say, "Let me continuously repeat Your name, think of You, feel that You are working through me every minute. Without You I cannot live. I cannot even breathe. I am completely in Your hands—like a little baby in the arms of the mother. If some difficulty comes, all I know is to cry. You know immediately why I am crying."

If we really want God, we don't have to do anything. Just cry. So in repeating the mantram, you are literally crying, calling God's name. You should have that sincere trust. Mere repetition brings benefit, but it will be many-fold if you do it with real feeling, with this total confidence.

30 November

SPIRITUAL PRACTICE IS NOT WHAT YOU ARE DOING, BUT WHAT YOU ARE THINKING

When you repeat your mantram, you should feel, "I'm not doing it for my sake. I am doing it to train my mind. If I train my mind, I can serve better." So even your mantra repetition becomes an offering. "I'm doing everything as an offering to God, guru and humanity." Then you don't make distinctions between, "Ahh, this is *sadhana* , this is spiritual practice. That is not." Sometimes we say, "Oh, I don't have time to do *sadhana.* I'm always working on the bulldozer." So what is bulldozing then? Your working on the bulldozer is not spiritual? Do you think that only by going into a corner and closing your eyes and murmuring something you are doing spiritual practice?

Spiritual practice is not what you are doing, but what you are thinking. Remember that. If you could understand the meaning of *sadhana* you would know how to do it. You don't have to change your activities and say, "This is *sadhana* but this is not." Even your eating. Even when you sit on the toilet you are doing *sadhana.* Remember that. Everything becomes a spiritual practice. We should transform all our activities into this kind of *sadhana.* That means "I am doing everything as a meditation, as an offering, as a prayer to serve God through service to the humanity." I wouldn't even say to humanity; do it as a service to the nature. Why only humanity? Humanity means only human beings. Serve the dogs, serve the cats, serve the rats, serve the mosquitoes. Serve the plants. Be nice to them, be loving. Even if you have to pull out a weed, do it in a loving way.

December

1 December

HE HAS GIVEN EVERYTHING POSSIBLE

There are three things that are very rare: a healthy human body, a desire to get liberated and a guide to help you. When you have all three, and waste them, God will not kindle you up or say, "Come on, wake up!" No. He has given you everything possible.

We have done a lot of meritorious deeds. We have gone through a lot of births and deaths. Whether you believe in reincarnation or not, it is a fact. You are not simply jumping into a human form right away. The soul has traveled a long way. You are almost at your journey's end: animal to human, human to superhuman. Unconscious to subconscious to conscious to superconscious. The Bhagavad Gita says that at the last minute, desire becomes very strong. Your very strong desires will come to the surface at the last minute, because at that time your body and mind—everything—is weak. You are already getting ready to leave, so everything is shattered. All the desires that have somehow been suppressed, but not annihilated, will be waiting there. All of a sudden the strongest desire will come up, and when the soul leaves the body, it goes with that desire. That is why we should be very, very careful about what desires we cultivate. There may be many other little desires, it doesn't matter; but our predominant desire should be something elevating. Something that would take you away from this to a higher level, never something that would take you backward.

So even if someone all of a sudden gives you a good spanking, you should say, "Hari OM!" Yes. If a thorn pricks you, "Hari OM!" If you get a shock, "Hari OM!" Develop that and you have a chance. Repeat the holy name always; not necessarily "Hari OM," but any holy name. When you wake up it should come with the waking. When you go to bed, it should go with you to bed. You have to cultivate that. You cannot say, "Ahh, I can easily develop it later on. Why should I bother about it now?" No. Make hay while the sun shines.

HAVE POSITIVE, POSITIVE, POSITIVE THOUGHTS

Whenever you get into any problem, remember: "I'm not the body, not the mind, immortal Self I am. I am Existence-Knowledge-Bliss Absolute!" Simply blow the depression away. It comes like a cloud and you can blow it away. Shout at the top of your voice, "I am blissful, I am joyful, I am easeful." You are nothing less than that. Ascertain your true nature. Don't constantly hypnotize yourself saying, "Oh, I am a mortal, I am a sinner, I am this, I am that." You're not. If you keep on thinking that way, you will become that. As you think, so you become. Think that you are great, you are great. Think that you are hopeless, certainly you will become hopeless. Don't give room for negative thinking. Always have positive, positive, positive thoughts.

People who pan for gold collect tons of crude rock. If they just saw the crudeness, they would throw it all away. Instead, their eye is on the few ounces of gold hidden within that rock. If you keep your eye on the gold, you won't get tired of cleaning the rock; and ultimately you will get the gold. Never lose sight of the gold in you. You might have accumulated a lot of dirt and dust. It doesn't matter. Take the time to clean it out. Keep your mind on the gold that you are looking for.

GIVE A HELPING HAND

It is of no use to blame or dislike others. If you don't like someone, you don't have to go near that person. But don't create problems for the person or condemn him or her either.

It is even better to try to find out why you don't like someone. Analyze it. You may not like certain things he or she does. Fine, but you should ask yourself, "Haven't I done the same thing before?" Maybe you have learned that lesson and you are not doing it now. The other person is still making that mistake, and will learn the lesson just as you did. Allow others to learn in their own time. Have compassion and understanding. When you think in this way, you stop disliking the person. You may even be able to help the person. But if you cannot, allow that one to take his or her own time to learn and grow.

We are not all at the same level. With the proper understanding, you will not have any difficulty in liking everyone. If you dislike someone, it's *your* mistake because you lack understanding. That person might be a terrible sinner who made a lot of mistakes, but your dislike is also a mistake. So if you cannot help the person, at least do not dislike him or her. You have probably done the same thing before but have just forgotten about it. People grow by making mistakes. That is why we should never hesitate to give more chances to people. Give a helping hand rather than a condemning one.

4 December

BY GIVING YOU NEVER LOSE

Give until it hurts, but do not lose your peace. It is all right not to help others if it will help you in preserving your own peace. If you are going to lose your peace, then how are you going to help others? When you are easeful and peaceful, then you can be useful. Otherwise, you may even harm rather than help the situation.

Do not do something if you know that by doing it you are going to disturb your peace. Maintaining your peace is more important. But at the same time, give as much as you can. Even if you get hurt, it doesn't matter. Give. Because by giving, you never lose. There is a joy in thinking of others first. You will have *more* peace and joy in doing that.

5 December

THE DOOR IS NEVER CLOSED UNTIL THE LAST LAME SHEEP COMES IN

Question: Are there some souls who will never merge with the Cosmic Consciousness in the end?

Sri Gurudev: All of the souls ultimately have to gain the same Cosmic Consciousness. The door is never closed until the last lame sheep comes in. We are all ultimately, ultimately going to go to the same place. There's no doubt about it. Only some may be swifter. Some use their intelligence and go on the straight road. Others jump a little here, a little there. But still the door is left open. It is never closed: "Oh, you are too late, you can't come in." No. God is a merciful Father. He will wait even for thousands of years, thousands of births.

6 December

THE SOUL ITSELF IS PURE CONSCIOUSNESS

Question: When the soul joins all other souls in its final chapter, does it retain a consciousness or is that lost?

Sri Gurudev: The soul itself is pure consciousness. So it retains its pure consciousness state, but it doesn't retain the individual consciousness that is part of the mind. Once you achieve that state, the product of the mind is gone, like a dream that is gone when you wake up. The mental consciousness constantly varies. All your ideas, thoughts, experiences are not stored in the Self, but in the mind. Here we should understand the difference between soul and Self. The soul is a mixture of Self and mind. Or, in other words, the soul is the Self reflected in the mind, the mental mirror. So it is a reflection of the Self that you call soul, and that seems to have all the colors and the modifications of the mind. But once you raise your level of consciousness to pure consciousness, then there is no mind at all. Along with the mind, all this mental dream goes away. You don't retain any of those old memories. But until that total liberation, you do retain them.

7 December

THERE'S NOTHING SERIOUS ABOUT IT

Life is a play. It was never meant to be a serious, heavy thing. Our own ego makes it that way. God just wanted to have some fun. That's why He created all of us. But we don't know His purpose behind it all, and so we seem to be missing all the fun. Just treat everything as play. All this coming and going, meeting, eating, welcoming, sending off, taking birth, saying goodnight and goodbye. It's all fun. We should see it in this light and take things easy. It's all a great, divine play and we all have our roles. Don't even say that we are playing our roles. We are all puppets; there is a wire tied to us. That wire is Cosmic Consciousness. We all have that Consciousness. Whatever that Consciousness thinks, we think. But when we fail to understand that, and allow our individual egos to come to the surface, we think that we are doing something. That is what you call basic ignorance. Actually we have no business of our own here at all. Nothing belongs to us. Not even these bodies, not even these minds. Just because we happen to have something in our hands, we immediately try to possess it. We say, "This is mine. I should keep it. I did it." Our "I" gets cataracted by too many "mines." If we could just perform an operation on that cataract, we would see better. So just leave it to the Lord. Then there's nothing serious about it.

8 December

DO NOT BE SERIOUS ABOUT ANYTHING

We cannot really save the world. We cannot even destroy the world. It is not in our hands. If that Supreme Power wanted to save the world, it wouldn't even take a second for it to happen. All of us could be saints and sages overnight. All He has to do is just think, "Come on all of you be saints," and that would be it. But He is not doing that. Instead, He is letting us be a little ignorant. That is His fun. You sometimes forget this and take life too seriously. At least when it gets too tough and you are really caught up in it all, at that point sit back and say, "It's all right." Don't be serious about anything, anything, anything. Just have fun.

Always keep this awareness of the Divine *Leela* or God's Play. If we just remember this, we won't be projecting our ego. How often we get caught in thinking, "I did it! I got it! I lost it!" For one week, try saying: "It's all God's fun. I'll simply do whatever He wants me to do." Have a sample week like this. You will feel very light. You will get the Light. Then if you like, you can continue. If not, take back your ego. It is always there.

NOTHING IS IMPOSSIBLE TO ACCOMPLISH

The entire life is based on imagination. In a way, you are also imagining in meditation. In meditation, you think of God. Have you ever seen God? No. So you are imagining, "That must be God. God should be like this. God should be like that." That is *your* God. Another person would imagine the same God in his or her own way. That is why even God's form varies according to the person who imagines God. That is the proof that everything comes from within.

In meditation you are imagining something that you want to ultimately become or develop. "God is almighty, God is all-powerful, God is all-forgiving, God is all love." You constantly think of certain things and the mind assumes that image, assumes that quality. But one thing is important: you should think *strongly*. You should be strong enough in your suggestions. That is what you are trying to develop in your meditation. You are strengthening your thoughts by constantly thinking of the same thing. To make yourself strong in your thoughts, you have to keep on dinning that into your mind. "This is what I want to become. This is what I want to become." That means you imagine that you are going to be like that—that you *are* that. Then certainly you *will* become that. Once you achieve that kind of thought power, nothing is impossible to accomplish.

10 December

EVEN YOUR LIVING IS YOUR IMAGINATION

Imagination is literally what you think, what kind of image you have about yourself and about others and about things. First comes self-image, and that image projects itself onto other things and creates imaginations. All of your imaginations depend upon your image, and your image is actually based on your experience of yourself. So it originates from within. That's why we say the entire world is your own projection. You project your image onto everything; everything is seen with your own vision. In that sense we are continuously imagining. Even your living is your imagination. Because you are imagining that you are alive, you are alive. If you seriously begin to imagine that you are dying little by little, you will die. It has been proven. If you seriously imagine that you are losing all of your strength, in half an hour you will collapse. It will happen. Always remember to think beautiful, positive thoughts. As you think, so you become.

THAT'S PROBABLY WHY IT'S CALLED A "DOUGHNUT"

We are all getting fried. Don't jump out of the pan before you get fried completely. Just be comfortable inside it. If you jump out of the pot, nobody will eat you. Who will eat a half-fried doughnut? That's probably why it's called a "doughnut — do-not jump out." So have complete trust in God; everything else will happen by itself. Your life will be smooth sailing. Let's not have unnecessary worry over anything. Yes, I know sometimes we are even worried about the future of the world, "What will happen? They are all piling up arms and ammunition and nuclear this and that." What are you going to accomplish with your worry? Worrying doesn't help. If you remain calm and peaceful, you will know what to do. Just do your part and leave the rest to God.

12 December

GO WITH FULL CONFIDENCE

Don't worry about anything. Worry never brings any benefit to anyone. On the other hand, it spoils even the little that you might do. There is a beautiful saying I read on a daily calendar page many years ago. It said, "Sorrow is nothing but what you borrow." Nobody is going to give you that. You go and borrow it. If you don't care to borrow it, there's no sorrow for you. That's all. You are the cause of your worry. Nobody can bring worry to you. If you care, decide not to worry. Remember, worry is not going to bring anything to us. On the other hand, it will sap away even the little energy, the little capacity, that we may have. A worried doctor cannot operate, you all know that. A worried student cannot write an exam. Go with full confidence. Just say, "I'm doing all that I can. That's it."

We make things change. Everything takes its own time. We are in a hurry to change things. We want everything instantaneously. Allow nature to have its say. Nature is God. Let our lives be filled with trust in the higher will. Whether it is an individual or an organization or a nation or the whole globe, let it go smoothly in its own time.

13 December

WHEN YOU REALIZE THAT, YOU WON'T EVEN WANT TO DO IT

Question: What can people do who have a tendency to judge themselves harshly or to look very negatively at themselves?

Sri Gurudev: The question is not about self-judgement, but about self-negativity, or having a poor opinion of yourself. Certainly, that will affect your heart, your mind and your personality. What you think you ultimately become. Don't we say that? "As you think, so you become." If you are thinking negatively about yourself, you don't need any negativity to come from somewhere else. You are negating yourself. So, you have to analyze it. "Is this good for me? Is it helpful for me to have these negative thoughts? Is it constructive or destructive? I become what I think. If my thoughts are like this, what will I become?" When you realize that, you won't want to do it anymore. Often people don't take it seriously; but your own negative thoughts *will* affect you. That's why, at least for our own sake, if not for the sake of others, we should not develop any negative thoughts about ourselves or about anybody else. No one interested in his or her own welfare, physical and mental, should invite negative thoughts.

In the same way, how does one find self-love? Love yourself. Think of that. "I am God's child. God has given me all these gifts. I love myself because God is functioning through me." Even if you have some disabilities, it doesn't matter; still you don't have to think that God doesn't love you. No. That's where the theory of karma comes in. You must have done something before that brought it to you. Think, "God is merciful so He is purging me of my karma by making me go through this." There *must* be a cause; nothing happens without a cause. So think of all these things, "Yes, God loves me. I'm the dear, dear child of God." Think of all the gifts that God has given you. You will learn to love God, and by loving God you will love yourself also.

FIND OUT THE SECRET

The first and foremost reason not to have jealousy is that it affects the person himself or herself. If you are jealous, it affects you physically and mentally. It in no way helps you or anyone else. So at least for your own sake, it is advisable not to have that. Every time you feel that kind of emotion, immediately think, "Is it not affecting me? And who is the cause of it? Myself! So at least for my own sake, I should stop it."

If you are jealous because you see someone else getting something that you are not getting, find out the reason. Why is that person getting all the attention or progressing, growing well in everything? What is the secret of that person's growth? Think of that, instead of simply feeling jealous. Find out his or her secret. Jealousy means that when others are doing well, you feel unhappy about it. If you really look into it, you might find that there is a nice, good attitude in their life. Maybe they are not running after things; they are contented with what they have. They have more faith, more devotion. They put themselves in the position to receive. By thinking of the good qualities of others, you will also develop them and your life will be so beautiful. Automatically when you feel that contentment, things will come to you by themselves. People will like you, appreciate you too.

IF YOU MEDITATE REGULARLY, YOU WILL HAVE NO COMPLAINTS IN LIFE

Meditation is very important if you want to practice any kind of yoga. You cannot become a good *karma yogi* without proper meditation, nor a good *bhakti yogi*. Meditation is the sustaining force. And don't say, "Ohh, if I come to meditation I can't fulfill my other obligations." Or, "I have to stay up late so I can't get up that early." These are all just excuses. They come out of the minds that do not know the importance of it. Meditation takes care of your body and mind *and* activities. So I would say that everybody should make a point of meditating. We need the mind. It is with the mind that we do everything. The mind is our key. If that key is not kept in good shape, how are you going to perform your duties? The one and only way to keep the mind in good shape, to keep the mind clean and sharp, is by meditation. So, make all the effort that's necessary to be regular in meditation.

If you meditate regularly, you will have no complaints in life. All of your problems would solve themselves if you were regular in your meditation. Through meditation, the mind gets the capacity to solve problems and rise above difficulties. The people who complain, "Oh, I am this, I am that, I don't get this, I don't get that. I feel this way, I feel that way, physically, mentally," who have constant complications, would find that it all could be easily burnt out by regular meditation. So please make no excuses for missing that.

EVERYBODY IS NEEDED

Only timid people get intimidated. If you don't want to be like that, don't compare yourself with others. You are what you are. Everybody is needed to make the whole drama, the cosmic play. Everybody. The king is needed, the queen is needed, the gatekeeper is needed, the hero is needed, the villain is needed, is it not so? A play has every role. Probably you are just acting your part. So if you are a gatekeeper standing in front of the gate while the king is sitting on the throne, why should you feel intimidated? Without you the play can't be enacted. It is only during the play that you are here and he is there. When the curtain falls, you embrace each other and laugh at it, "Hey, you did very well playing the part of a king." We all have to play our roles.

What is unimportant in this world? Nothing. God has never created anything that is unimportant. If you think, "I am also equally God's child. He created me like this. I am happy to be like this," how can anyone intimidate you? It's your own wrong notion about yourself. You think little of yourself. You don't think you are potentially divine. You don't think that you are the child of God, created by God. If you are a lion cub, and if you forget that and bleat like a lamb, who can help you? Rise up, exert your birthright, affirm your true nature: "I am that I am. I am nothing less than God, my Father." Then even if someone says, "Hey, you are a fox," you will say, "Maybe that's what you see. I know I am a lion." Yes. That's what. Realizing the true nature of the Self will take you away from all these problems. You are the same always, eternally. You are that immortal soul. Nothing less than that. All other things are just temporary. That is what you call the highest knowledge.

DO EVERYTHING AS AN INSTRUMENT IN THE HANDS OF GOD

Question: What is the best way of disciplining oneself to complete a task?

Sri Gurudev: Know that it is God's task. God wants you to do that, so He is giving you the interest, the capacity and the knowledge to do it. If you think of yourself as an instrument in the hands of God, you will always succeed in whatever you do. You will always do a better job. But if you project your ego and say, "*I* am doing it," then you get into problems. That means you want people to pat you on your shoulder and say, "Ahh, you did it very well." And if they don't, you won't do it the next time. Instead, do everything as an instrument in the hands of God.

THERE IS AN UNSEEN GUIDE BEHIND EVERYTHING

Don't be concerned with how to set priorities in your service. When your mind is clean and neutral and you are selflessly serving, you will be able to hear your own conscience telling you what is to be done first.

Priority depends on urgency as well as your own capabilities. If someone has just been hit by a car, do you need to worry about your priorities? Obviously you will do what you can to help the person or to get help. If your mind is clean, the right actions will be presented to you right away. There is a higher intelligence that will tell you *immediately* what to do. Just follow that direction.

There is an unseen Guide behind everything. Let that Guide guide us. If nothing comes to mind right away, pause a minute and ask, "God, what am I to do?" The answer will come. But remember not to use your personal interest in any situation. Stay neutral, then you will know the right thing to do. That is very, very important in deciding priorities.

HOW DO YOU KNOW THAT YOU HAVE NOT SEEN HIM?

Question: I have a growing desire to see God. It has become the thing I want most. But no matter how much I long for Him, my worldly duties and needs get in the way. Can you help me?

Sri Gurudev: How do you know that you have not seen Him? I heard Him saying, "I have been in front of this person so many times, but he never even recognized Me. He was calling, calling, calling for Me. So I went there many times, stood right in front of him, and he didn't even bother to look at Me. He just brushed Me aside and kept on saying, 'God, where are You? Where are You?'"

Before you look for God, you should know what He looks like, or at least what God is. God has no particular form, but He appears in all forms and names. It is with His consciousness that I am saying all these things; and with His consciousness, you are listening. To simplify it, we say that God is all consciousness—superconsciousness, cosmic consciousness—or peace. God is already there in you as peace, but you disturb your peace by searching for God. Stop searching and disturbing your peace, and you will experience God. A disturbed mind can never understand God. Looking for God is not our first and foremost duty. Our first and foremost duty is to take care not to let the mind lose its peace. You don't have to *make* the mind peaceful. If you leave it alone, it is peaceful. In our own lives we should see that we don't lose our peace due to our thoughts, words, actions.

Learn to remain undisturbed, unshakeable, as steady as the Rock of Gibraltar. You should treasure the peace of your mind so much that nothing, nothing, nothing would shake you. You should be ready to renounce anything and everything that is going to disturb your peace. Name, fame, money, power, position, relatives, friends—all should be secondary to maintaining your peace. Everything else is nothing compared to peace of mind. With that peace, you will easily see God.

20 December

SOMETIMES YOU LISTEN

Question: Who is *Satchidananda* or what is *Satchidananda*?

Sri Gurudev: In a way, everyone is *Satchidananda*. Every thing is *Satchidananda*. Don't think that *Satchidananda* is just the name of one person. All that we see is the form, and there is a name to go with that form. So the differences we see are only in the forms and the names. But if you go a little deeper inside, behind the forms and names, what is it that has taken on this appearance? That essence is what you call *Satchidananda*. Even that is divided into three: *Sat, chid, ananda*. What is *sat* ? Truth, existence. What is. That is *sat*. That means the essential reality, the truth, or the existence. *Chid* is knowledge. And *ananda* is bliss. Existence, knowledge, bliss. That means the knowledge of the existence or the existing one; the Truth reveals itself. Knowledge of that. And then by knowledge comes bliss.

Sat-chid-ananda is the common name for all of us, and for everything also. The Self within you is *Satchidananda*. It directs you continuously. It advises you. Sometimes you listen. We should *always* listen to that Self.

21 December

MY ONLY WISH

Question: If you had a wish, what would it be?

Sri Gurudev: My only wish is to be a good instrument in the hands of that Supreme Entity that you call God. All these years He has kept me under His feet, used me as an instrument, and has taken care of me so that I wouldn't get involved in any ego problems. And I wish that He would continue to do that. That's my only wish. Other than that, there's nothing else. I may say, "I wish you all health and happiness," but that's in your hands. If a wish comes like that, even that is His wish being expressed through this instrument. So, "Let Thy Will be done."

IF YOU WANT TO EXPERIENCE GOD IN YOUR LIFE

Just close your eyes and think for a minute, "Does the whole world love me? How many people don't love me? How many animals don't love me? How many plants don't love me?" Then you will know yourself how healthy and happy you are.

God is love. That is the essential teaching from all the scriptures. If we want to experience God, we should express that love in our life, just as God loves everything and everybody. God loves a rat, a cat, a dog, a donkey, a pig, a sinner, a saint, an idiot, a scholar. The most beautiful and the most ugly. A good dancer. The one who doesn't even know how to walk.

No matter what you are and how you are, you see that unconditional love from God. God never said, "I will love you if only you do this, if only you are like that." No. Loving without limitations is "universal love." And that is God. If you want to experience that God in your life, love everything and everybody as God would love. Unconditionally.

Show the same love to one and all. Let nothing get harmed, hurt, or pained, even by your thought. It is possible to develop a life like that. We want everybody to love us, and we don't want anybody to hate us. In the same way, everybody would want that. Do unto others as you yourself would want it to be done unto you.

Spiritual teaching is very simple. Whether you repeat your mantram or not, whether you practice hatha yoga or not, whether you learn all the scriptures by heart or not, who worries about that? But, do you have unconditional love in your life? If you have that, you have everything.

At least during these beautiful holy days of Hannukah, Christmas, New Year's, and Deepavali, let us reaffirm ourselves to lead a life filled with love. That will take care of everything else.

CHRIST IS ALWAYS THERE

Question: Please speak about the second coming. Some people say that Christ is now in the world in a physical manifestation.

Sri Gurudev: In the Bhagavad Gita, Lord Krishna says clearly, "Whenever there is too much unrighteousness in the world, I come to educate people." That teacher is what you call an *avatar* or divine incarnation. When such an incarnation comes, nobody can keep it hidden. It will be made known to all. But the name and form will not necessarily be the same each time. That's where many people make a mistake. They look for another person exactly like Jesus, even in appearance. But it need not be that way. Sometimes you cannot easily recognize such an incarnation until you see the great qualities expressed in his or her life. But that doesn't mean that we are not helped until a great *avatar* comes and is revealed to the world.

God's spirit is always there. Christ is always there in spirit. He may even be seen in some other name, some other form. The great incarnations come mainly when the whole world is in trouble, and everyone really looks for that help and prays. Other than that, individually you may come across your second comings. The spirit never leaves us alone and goes somewhere, waiting for another time to come. To the spirit, there is no coming or going. It's only an expression. God never comes and never goes. God is. And God is omnipresent. From where would He come? Can He leave one place and go to another where He is not? No. When you are ready, God is there. You may call it the "second coming," but in truth God comes every second.

24 December

IF YOU ARE HUNGRY, TAKE IT, EAT IT

Every second God is coming, but we don't recognize Him. How many years went by before Jesus was recognized? By the time Mohammed and Buddha were recognized, half of their lives were gone. So it is up to us to recognize the spirit. Spirit is always ready, eagerly waiting to help us. We should not always limit it to a certain particular name and form. That's *our* limitation. Just because you believe in one name, one form, don't totally deny all the others. "Unless he comes in that form, I won't believe." Then who is the loser? You are the loser. It doesn't matter whether you are served food on china, or on silver, or on a leaf, or even in your hand; if you are hungry, take it, eat it. All these names and forms are just vehicles. Let us rise above all this and trust in that spirit.

25 December

EVERY DAY WILL BE YOUR CHRISTMAS

"Lord, You are the Light of Lights. You are the source of all lights. You are the Sun of Suns, Moon of Moons, Star of Stars. You are the light within and without. You are the Light of the enlightened. Kindly lead us from the darkness of ignorance to the light of understanding to realize the truth behind all these names and forms." This is my prayer on this holy occasion.

Every holy day should remind us of our inherent divine nature. At least on that holy day we should forget all of the man-made differences, even the differences that are seen in nature, and rise above these differences to recognize our spiritual oneness.

Don't just run after things. Look within. Experience that joy, that peace, that Jesus, that Moses, that Allah, that Mohammed, that Buddha. Use any name you want. That's my sincere wish for you. Think of that. Let this holy day bring this light into you so that you can celebrate Hannukah, Christmas, New Year, all the holy days all the time. You don't need to depend on a calendar, certain months, certain days, certain years. Every day will be your Christmas. Every day you will be receiving gifts through your chimney. Santa Claus will be there with you always.

> When the man begins to sight the glorious inner light,
> He drops all ego's fight, and knows the mission right,
> Does everything in delight and ever simply feels light.

May the Light of Lights light our lives. May the light of Hannukah be lit within you. May the Christ light be born in you. May the New Year dawn in you and bring a new life in the spirit. May this holy season inspire you with peace and joy. May God be with you.

26 December

POVERTY IS IN THE HEART

Poverty is in the heart. You don't own anything because you didn't bring anything with you when you came, and you are not going to take anything with you when you go. It is all given to you by God. When you have emptied your mind of ownership, that is renunciation or poverty. I will give you a small illustration.

Once King Janaka was studying under a great sage. He used to leave the palace and go to the hermitage and sit with all the other students to study the scriptures under the guidance of a swami. It seemed to the other students, however, that the teacher was treating the king a little specially. Naturally they became jealous, so they were gossiping. The sage knew what was happening, but he allowed it to continue for a while.

Ordinarily in those days in the hermitages the swamis used to sit and teach under a tree. One hermitage happened to be on the outskirts of the king's palace. One day the swami created the illusion that the palace was on fire. The ministers and servants from the palace came running saying that the palace was on fire and the fire was spreading. Immediately all the students got up and ran; but Janaka, the king himself, was just sitting there contemplating on what the teacher was saying. The swami was talking about the steadiness of the spirit, and Janaka was contemplating on that. He didn't even hear what was happening.

So all the other students got up and ran. After a few minutes though, they all came back saying, "It was just a false alarm. There is no fire at all. We don't know what happened." The swami said, "Ahh, is that all? Thank God! Okay, sit. But when the palace was on fire, why did you people run to put the fire out? The palace is far away. Are there not people there to do those things?" "Oh, no, we weren't worried about the palace. But our loincloths were hanging on a line very close to the palace, so we just ran there to save them." "I see. Do you know who is the owner of the palace?" "Yes, this strange man; he didn't even notice. He was just sitting here the whole time." Then the teacher said, "You see, you were attached to your loincloths and ran to save them, whereas he just sat here. He didn't even run to save his palace. So who is rich here, and who is poor? All you renunciates have is a loincloth. But he doesn't even have that much. *He* is really the poor man. Nothing can shake him."

King Janaka simply answered, "Well, there are people there to take care of it. This is a precious moment for me, why should I go?" Then the others realized how attached they were and got the lesson. It's not possessions that make you rich. Even attachment to a begging bowl can make you a householder; whereas you can have a big family and still be a renunciate. It's the attachment that makes the difference. So we should learn to empty our minds of the attachment, not of the things.

27 December

BORN FREE

You are *ever* free. Born free. Why do people feel the need to have "free time" or vacation time? Whatever you do you are doing freely if you have the right attitude. A true spiritual seeker should not discriminate between "free" days and "work" days. Learn to play even while you work. Work is worship. Work is play.

Have fun always. You should never be feeling tense or that you are working so hard that you need a vacation. Let your vacation be simply a change of work. Real freedom is enjoying whatever you do.

The whole of life is a drama. You are watching a continuous, constant, unending movie. In that process, if you want to go out on a day off and see a movie go through a projector, go ahead and do it. It's a change of activity, that's all.

Whatever you do, play your part well and enjoy it.

28 December

WHAT YOU CALL RELIGION

You are all looking for that God whose name is happiness, and your righteous approach to that happiness is what you call religion. If you approach that happiness without hurting yourself and hurting others, you are a religious person. But if you are trying to get happiness by hurting yourself or others, it's not religious.

29 December

LEAVE IT TO THE HIGHER AUTHORITY

Live in the golden present. Always feel, "Yes, this is my present, right now. The past is past. The future is not in our hands." Probably someone will ask, "Then should we not plan for tomorrow?" Yes, you should plan; but you should not worry about it. Ideas come, all right, plan. But know that there is someone who is going to approve or disapprove. Leave the final decision to the higher authority and be ready for anything. If you want to plan something for tomorrow, do it for the fun of planning today. But always remember that there is a final authority. The individual proposes, God disposes. That is life.

30 December

SOMETHING IN US SEEMS TO KNOW THAT GOD IS WITHIN

You are not going to *get* God. You are not going to surrender yourself to God. You are not even going to allow God to function through you. He is already doing that. All you have to do is know it. If you don't know, then you think that *you* are doing it. So as long as you think that *you* are doing something, let your conscience, which is part of God, guide you. Listen within; it will direct you. It will tell you what is right and what is wrong, what to do and what not to do. It is always there to guide you. Nobody is without that.

Something in us seems to unconsciously know that God is within. The guidance should come from within. That means you have to close your eyes, close your ears, close your senses to the world outside. Everyone should take at least a little time every day to sit and listen to the inner guidance. Sincerely ask: "Lord, tell me what to do. I know You are guiding me. Give me the strength and capacity to listen to You and to follow You. My contact with the outside world through the senses is not really helping me. It's making me more and more miserable." It's very true. Sensual experiences will literally take you away from the inner experience. All our miseries come due to our sensual experiences. We are satisfying our senses in every way possible. Feeding the senses means the ego becomes bigger and bigger. That's where discipline comes in. If you let loose everything, you can't achieve anything in life. We don't say that you should not enjoy the experience of the senses, but do so in a well-disciplined way. There should be a limitation to everything.

31 December

WHEN YOU GET GOD, YOU WON'T BE FILLING YOUR STOMACH WITH ICE CREAM

The kind of realization we talk about—that nothing outside can bring fulfillment to you—is only theoretical. You have heard of it, but mere theoretical knowledge is not enough. To experience it, you must convince your mind. Think of your past experiences outside. Analyze them. Did they bring you inner experience? Did they bring you satisfaction, or were they only borrowed: they came and now they are gone? At the same time, remember what inner experience is.

What do you want to experience within? A little fun? A nice taste? Inner experience does not mean, "I must just experience the taste of vanilla ice cream without eating it." You can't experience vanilla ice cream without eating it, but you *can* experience the pleasure of eating vanilla ice cream. What is that? Satisfaction. "Ahh, I *wanted* vanilla ice cream, that want created an urge, we went there and got it." So you wanted it, you got it, you ate it, and then, "Ahh, I got vanilla ice cream." You experienced the vanilla ice cream and thus you experienced your happiness, your satisfaction. But before you wanted the ice cream you were satisfied. You were contented. The minute you thought of the ice cream you lost your contentment. You went there, got it, and got back your contentment. If you keep that contentment always, whether you get it or not, that is inner experience. The inner experience is not based on anything outside. Seek the kingdom of God, and everything else just follows. When I say everything follows that does not mean literally every *thing* will follow. When you get God, you won't be filling your stomach with ice cream. But you will get the contentment of having eaten a gallon of ice cream without eating it. The contentment, not the taste.

The Reverend Sri Swami Satchidananda

The Reverend Sri Swami Satchidananda (Sri Gurudev) is one of the most revered living Yoga Masters of our time. A much-loved teacher, well known in today's world for his combination of practical wisdom and spiritual insight, he has given his life to the service of humanity, demonstrating by his own example the means of finding abiding peace within one's life and within one's self. His message of peace inside all people and harmony among all faiths and countries has been heard worldwide. Each year Sri Gurudev receives hundreds of invitations to speak at conferences, colleges, medical groups and houses of worship of all religions around the globe.

Born to a devout family in South India in 1914, Sri Gurudev spent his early years studying and working in fields as diverse as agriculture and electronics. He was successful in all of them. Yet he chose to give up a personal life for a life dedicated to inner peace, spiritual knowledge and communion with God. He studied with some of India's greatest saints and sages: among them, Sri Ramana Maharshi, Sri Aurobindo and his own spiritual master, the world-renowned Sri Swami Sivanandaji Maharaj of Rishikesh, Himalayas.

When Swami Satchidananda was asked to serve in Sri Lanka, it was not long before the first Satchidananda Ashram was founded by students who wanted to learn more from him. He spent thirteen years among them. In 1966 he was invited to visit the West, where his deep spiritual realization made a profound and lasting impression. Once again, he was soon surrounded by sincere students inspired to follow in his footsteps, and today there are Satchidananda Ashrams and Integral Yoga® Institutes, based on his teachings, throughout the world.

Sri Gurudev has sponsored innumerable ecumenical symposiums, retreats and worship services all over the world. During several private audiences, H.H. Pope Paul VI praised these efforts to promote interfaith activities. Sri Gurudev continues to travel around the world advocating harmony and meeting with spiritual and governmental leaders and other dignitaries, among them: H.H. Pope John Paul II, The Dalai Lama, Indira Gandhi, Mother Teresa and U Thant. He has traveled several times to the Soviet Union in an effort to encourage harmonious dialogue between the American and Russian people and to promote world peace. He has received many honors for his service, including the Martin Buber Award for Outstanding Service to Humanity, the B'nai B'rith Anti-Defamation League's Humanitarian Award; the titles of: Fellow of World Thanksgiving, Honorary Fellow of the World Vegetarian Congress and Fellow of Concordia University.

Sri Gurudev himself does not belong to any one faith, group or country. Dedicated to the principle that "Truth is One, Paths are Many," he goes wherever he is asked to serve, bringing together people of all backgrounds and beliefs to learn respect for all the different paths and to realize their common spirit and the universality of their goal. He has long dreamed of a permanent place where all can come together to individually realize that one Truth behind all the names and forms. The LOTUS (Light Of Truth Universal Shrine) is such a place. Opened in July 1986, the Shrine—inspired and designed by Sri Gurudev—is located in the United States at Satchidananda Ashram—Yogaville in Virginia. It is dedicated to the light of all faiths and to world peace and stands as a beautiful example of the universal teachings of Sri Swami Satchidananda.